CAMINO
MYSTERIES

ELENA SKVIRSKI

Camino Mysteries

Copyright © 2020 by Elena Skvirski
All rights reserved.

No part of this book may be reproduced in any form or by any electronic or mechanical means including information storage and retrieval systems, without permission in writing from the author. The only exception is by a reviewer, who may quote short excerpts in a review.

Contributions by Philip Szeremeta
Cover Image by Jetlaunch
Author Photo by Timothy Devine

Printed in the USA

First Printing: February 2020

Published by: Adventure Camino Publishing
www.AdventureCamino.com
Denver, Colorado

DEDICATION

This book is dedicated to my grandmother, Alla, who always achieves the impossible.

ACKNOWLEDGEMENTS

Thanks to all who helped me along the path and inspired this journey. This book is one of the gifts of creativity that Camino inspired in me. My hope is that it prompts others to explore the wonders of the Camino to advance their personal transformations.

CAMINO MYSTERIES

1. Camino Dreams   1
2. Pilgrim talk   15
3. Tiger   21
4. Long journey ahead   25
5. Cobblestone path   38
6. Lost in the forest   42
7. Waiting to be born   49
8. Dragonfly   54
9. Arriving at the Temple   61
10. Gifts of treasure   70
11. Beauty within   76
12. Together at last   80
13. Dragons in armor   85
14. Been there, done that   95
15. Loving the enemy   107
16. Precious message   114
17. Santiago on the horizon   122
18. Ending the quest   131
19. Who are you?   141
20. End of the world   146
21. Home sweet home   153

CAMINO DREAMS

"Meow!" Tiger rubbed against Stella's hand.

She rolled over and stretched. "Oh, Tiger, it's too early." Not that it mattered to Tiger. "I know, I know you want your morning treat. Such a pampered cat." Stella rubbed Tiger's gray head, scratched behind his ears and kissed his cold nose. She pulled her hand down his fluffy neck and back rubbing deep into the silky undercoat of the large, boxy and chunky cat. "You're not as fluffy as you think with your long fur. You've got a good bit of fat under those dark gray and black stripes." She made sure to give extra attention to each stripe along the flexible back of her feline companion who was purring in delight. "I bet you're a Maine coon cat… the way you hunt, disappear and come back with all those mice." Stella ruffled Tiger's long fluffy tail.

Stella yawned and rolled over. "That'll teach me to stay up late. But I love sitting on the roof listening to the pilgrims' stories and looking at the stars." She leaned on her elbow, rubbed her eyes and looked around her room. She loved the apple green color on the walls, somehow, they gave her an extra boost of energy. Kind of like the tangy taste and crunch of real apples. She would have loved the room in pink, her favorite color. But since she had to share the room with her younger brother, Artur, she had to compromise. Not that she minded. Besides, the poster above her bed with the *pink* and purple hydrangea bushes along a stony path added her personality to the room. It worked well with the picture of three birds sitting on a branch above Artur's bed. Only a stuffed toy bunny rabbit was in his bed now, covered by a dinosaur blanket. That was Artur, always up early but asleep before the first star was out. She grinned, wondering what small mischief her partner in crime was planning for the day.

Tiger rolled around, stretched out his paws and presented his belly for scratching and meowed again. "Okay, okay, Geesh, be patient." Stella slid to the edge of the bed and stood on the soft faux fur pink rug, letting the cozy softness mesh between her toes, and remembered last night. One of the things she enjoyed most about living in her parents' guesthouse was listening to the people talk about their walk on the *Camino de Santiago*. People had been walking this route for many centuries, looking for 'Camino magic' whatever that was. One day she'd figure out how to find it. No time to think about that now. Time to dress and get ready for the fun sunny day inviting her out with the chirping of the birds on the windowsill. She picked out a simple peachy-pink dress with small ruffles along the shoulders. Avoiding wearing shoes when she could, her light bare feet pattered on the painted wooden floorboards, and she headed downstairs. "Come on, Tiger, let's get that treat." Tiger meowed, jumped off the bed and followed. "You know we're going to find that 'Camino Magic' one of these days," she whispered.

"Morning, Mama!" Stella reached up and kissed her mother's cheek, taking in a faint scent of lilac. How she reveled in those hugs in the morning, holding mom's face with both hands and looking at the dark hair framing her face and those caring almond shaped eyes. Mom's hazel green eyes came from her great-grandmother. Her older brother, Philip, got them too. While Stella inherited her height and skinny figure from both her parents, her strawberry blond hair resembled her aunt Tanya's. The hot summer sun added brighter streaks of blond to Stella's flighty hair. The more time she or Artur spent outside, the more they looked like siblings with their deep brown eyes, lighter hair and effects of the summer setting in, making it hard to tell if it was tan on their olive skin or dust they acquired roaming around all day. The kids didn't look much like their parents, maybe they came from the stars or the cabbage patch.

"Good morning, honey." Mama leaned down and squeezed Stella's slender body in a tender hug, while bracing herself at the same time for the impact of Tiger's hello rub against her leg. The giant cat was so friendly. Sometimes she could lose balance if he made contact in just the right spot below her knee as he arched his back and brushed against it. "There's a lot to do today. More guests are coming tonight."

"Yum, something smells good. Did you make cinnamon rolls again? Tiger, give me some space on the bench, you cuddle monster!"

"Apple cinnamon pancakes, just like your grandma made for me." Mama set a plate on the table. "Artur and dad were hungry. Artur eats like a champ, glad there were some left. He was up way early collecting acorns and pinecones for some grand slingshot project he wanted to tell you about. They're off in the garden now. Guests will be coming down soon, maybe you guys can move that projectile material pile a little to the side. Will you take care of the front desk again?"

"You know I will, Mama! I love greeting everyone and giving them your freshly baked pastries. Everyone's so friendly." Stella dug into her pancakes. "These are delicious, thanks for saving some for me!"

Later that day, while her parents straightened up the house and yard, Stella roamed around with Tiger and Artur. What fun to climb the trees to pick fruit or dig in the dirt for veggies from the garden. They usually couldn't wait for things to ripen and chomped down on produce others considered too sour or too green. What was it like to walk the Camino, she wondered while she sat on the front porch by the rose bush, watching the pilgrims and smacking her lips at the tasty fresh apple. Stella laughed at Tiger when he ran around chasing flies and grasshoppers. Yet it was the pilgrims who held her attention. Many of them waved to her as they walked past.

Some walked alone, some in pairs, others in small groups. All different ages and origins. Many were Spaniards whom she understood. She did live in a village in Spain after all. Others must have come from far away since they looked different, and she couldn't understand what they said. Not that it mattered, they still greeted her or smiled. There were the youngsters walking with their families too; the young children were being pushed in strollers or carried. Oh, how she envied the older kids! They must be having a grand adventure, she guessed. She'd give anything to join them. Though some needed encouragement and their parents reminded them ice-cream and treats waited in the next town.

Tiger climbed into her lap, and she petted his soft fur as he purred. Her older brother Philip got to walk the Camino for the first time when he was twelve. Why couldn't she go at the age of seven? "It's not fair, I've seen plenty even younger," Stella whispered. "They wouldn't even have to bribe me with ice cream or *pulpo*. Even though I love the small pieces of boiled octopus sprinkled with olive oil, salt, and paprika pepper, I wouldn't complain the way Mama said Philip did before. Nope, nothing would make me happier." Stella sighed. "Someday, Tiger. Some day."

How she wished she'd been with their parents back then. They'd been quite captivated and inspired by the Camino. Only a few years later they relocated to this quaint village in Spain, right along the walking path for the pilgrims. Stella loved the old abandoned farm with the large stone house her parents had purchased. They'd converted a portion to cozy sleeping quarters for the pilgrims. Philip was gone to the university now, so it was just her, Artur and Tiger roaming on the farm in the summers. Papa jokingly hinted that Mama may have overdone it just a bit planting so many rosebushes around the property, but Stella loved the effervescent fragrance and bright colors around her.

Taking in a big breath, she filled her lungs and her whole body with the lively essence coming from the rose buds. She settled back down on the step to observe the kaleidoscope of people and colors on the Camino.

"Hi, what's your name?" Two girls of about twenty stopped for refreshment across the path where a small rock was fashioned into a natural fountain long ago to capture the natural spring coming out of the ground.

"Hi. I'm Stella, what are your names?"

"I'm Louise, this is my friend Erica. So, what are you up to today?" The girl took off her hat and wiped her forehead with the back of her hand.

"Well, I just finished target shooting a big bale of hay, but the slingshot was the first one my brother made, and bull's eye is safe. All the other circles are safe too." Stella showed them the crude slingshot. "In fact, the whole bale is safe, not a single acorn hit it."

"Can I see it?" Louise extended her palm and Stella placed it carefully, quite flattered that an adult took interest in the kids' escapades. "Well, he did a great job, maybe you guys just need some practice. I mean a *lot* of practice to make it work correctly. Just don't give up."

"Oh, we have plenty of time for practice here on the farm." She grinned.

"You know, chatting here with you reminds me of the time I spent with my cousin at our grandma's farm in the summers." Erica took a swig of the water and closed her eyes as it touched her lips. This water is almost as good as the wine from the fountain we passed earlier on the Camino."

Stella wasn't sure if their story was real or also part of the Camino magic. She stepped closer and tilted her head a little. "What kinds of things did you do?"

"One time, our imagination ran a little wild." Erica's eyes got that distant look, and little wrinkles appeared in the corners as she squinted, barely holding back laughter. "We were walking near a field where a herd of cows grazed and lay around. A group of calves pushed and shoved each other." She snorted while trying to get the story out. "The bull stood steady, on the lookout nearby, following each of our movements with his blood-filled eyes, making sure we kept a safe distance from his proteges. We made our way on the side of the meadow. Well, all of a sudden, he moved his head just so sharply and bent it with the horns down and snorted. That was our cue! We took off and ran for our lives."

Louise covered her mouth and let out a small yelp. Stella was about to ask something, but the words never came out.

"We saw a tree up ahead with one branch a little out of reach, but we knew we had to try anyway. Jumping and grabbing on to the trunk, we scrambled up that saving tree." Erica flailed her arms. "I was up first, yelling to my cousin, "Come on! Quick! Get up here!" Finally, we both got up high and safe, trying to catch our breath! Panting and wiping our foreheads, we dared to look down at the raging bull. But… To our surprise, there was no bull under the tree, or nearby on the path. He still stood there with all the cows in the meadow. Hadn't moved an inch!"

Louise spewed the water from her mouth. Little droplets shimmered in the air and landed on her hiking boots. Stella plopped down on the stone bench and rolled around in bouts of laughter. Tears rolled down her cheeks as she held her belly. "So… you mean… the bull… wasn't going… to gore you to death…"

"Still here to tell the story! Though, we had some explaining to do why our jackets had scrapes and tears on them." Erica filled up her bottle and screwed on the cap.

Louise caught her breath, wiped her mouth and face. Erica beamed as she picked up her pack, flung it around her back as if it was full of feathers and adjusted her floppy hat. "Well, enjoy your day, Stella. Fun chatting with you."

"Bye!" Stella yelled after them. "Come back again." And just like that they were gone on to the next village or maybe farther. Oh, how she wished she could go with them and hear more stories.

In the afternoon, she saw a group of walkers, some with already silver hair and trekking poles for balance and support. Some walked with their eyes fixed on the ground and far away in their thoughts, sometimes stumbling on a rock and looking around like they just woke up from a deep sleep. Some chatted with the others, some walked and whistled or sung under their breath. Voices of the stragglers in the back sounded weary but lightened up as one man recounted some story using exuberant gestures and facial expressions. "Look, the fountain, perfect time for a drink and rest!" His voice rang out with relief, especially after his companions of different body types, fitness levels and physical abilities normalized their breathing. After drinking their fill, they marched on, almost in unison, and their steps echoed with laughter still audible for some time.

Later on, a middle-aged couple inched their way up to the fountain. The lady leaned on her trekking pole favoring the foot on the opposite side as she gently placed it on the ground with each step. They filled their water bottles in no particular rush and plopped down on the stone bench. As if on demand, Stella's neighbor guided a herd of sheep and caused a small roadblock with his bleating river of beige and dusty-white wool flowing down the street. The couple snapped photos with their smartphones in pure delight, and watched the sheep advance all the way down the street.

Well after the sounds of the bells faded, the husband got up, stretched his back and rubbed his neck. The wife massaged her foot and stared at the shoe still on the bench next to her. Her eyes wandered around, glanced over the path with some hesitation and suddenly focused on the sign above the front door of Stella's guesthouse. The husband followed the direction of his wife's glance. With the unspoken harmony of a long-term couple, they greeted Stella with "Buenas dias!" almost at the same time. The question followed about available space for them to sleep in the house. Stella welcomed them in with a smile. At the desk, she pressed a small rubber stamp into the ink pad and stamped their pilgrim passports.

"Nice image!" The wife examined the booklet and followed Stella upstairs to a large room with sets of bunk beds covered in crisp white sheets and soft blankets.

Each person carried a pilgrim's passport to be stamped each day as proof of walking the distance. They could get stamps in any café or restaurant or a place they slept. Stella's family guesthouse had an image of Tiger sitting on his hind legs near a path and looking very suave. At the end of the walk, in the cathedral of Santiago de Compostela, pilgrims received a certificate of completion of their journey. Mama and Papa showed her theirs from various paths they walked.

"Those were the amazing times we had on the Camino." They reminisced examining the dates and images of each stamp and told the children special stories from their travels. Even her name Stella was related to Compostela, which in Latin means "field of stars." They carried her and Artur in a backpack or a stroller with them on the Camino from six months old, but both were too young to remember. Now, running a guesthouse occupied too much of their time. Stella wished they could get a break sometimes so she could taste those adventures too.

In their determined journey to Santiago, pilgrims left comments in their guestbook in many different languages.

"Thank you for your hospitality, great space to contemplate and ponder, Gene M."

"*Grateful for the welcome in your cozy home. Your family inspires us to keep walking the Way, Cathy, Australia.*"

"*Loved celebrating our 25th wedding anniversary in the company of amazing pilgrims in your home, Josh and Kate, Colorado.*"

"*Thanks for making our stay comfortable and restful. We walked about 20 kilometers yesterday (12 miles) and probably will double that tomorrow since we got awesome rest! Miguel, Barcelona.*"

* * *

Stella and Artur inspected the map and found the countries mentioned in the comments from all corners of the world: many European countries, South and North America, Asia, Australia, even Africa. Some didn't sign the book, but she remembered their smiles and their gestures of gratitude for her family's hospitality. "This was a great place to hang out. Wish we could have stayed for more than one night, but you know, the trail calls." Patrick, one of a young group of Irish students teased. It was fun for her and Artur to be included in their dynamic game of soccer after which the young appetites requested extra helpings of the homemade stew.

Each morning after breakfast, folks kept walking forward, in unity with their backpacks, some smaller and some larger. Those with large packs seemed to be so burdened and their pace was somewhat hampered by all their possessions they carried around all day. No detail from the stream of people and backpacks escaped Stella's inquisitive eyes. Each passerby carried their story, and she could read it as they passed. One young man walked in jeans and sneakers with his school backpack. Stella guessed he was from somewhere in Europe and started walking on a whim, picking up his things last minute without much preparation. His phone rang as he was passing, "You won't believe where I am. On the Camino in Spain! I just hopped on the train last Saturday and here I am!" So much joy flowed from his impromptu decision.

Sometimes men or women in their late 60's passed. They sported t-shirts that seemed a little faded on the shoulders, backpacks with some splatters of dried up mud on the bottom, tall dusty hiking boots supporting the ankles and wide brimmed hats protecting their faces and necks. "They must be the retirees who walked over the Pyrenees from the French border." Stella heard many started their Way there. "It must have rained in the mountains. I bet it took them over a month or more to walk all the way from there, but they have time. They worked so hard coming up, now they can enjoy the leisurely walk," she relayed the story to Tiger. The cat often curled up next to her, raising his watchful eye from time to time if he heard loud voices. Artur wasn't too keen on sitting still and watching the pilgrims. He preferred building some contraptions for feeding the chickens and the goats or collected fresh grass and dug out carrots for the rabbits of the farm.

A young couple had a different pace from everyone on the trail one day. They appeared all fresh with brightly colored new gear and unspoiled hiking shoes. The young woman took it all in with her wide-open eyes. Every stone house, every landmark, every stone church resulted in a sigh, a squeal and a photo for the book of their Camino memories. "Look at the storks and their nest on the church steeple! Never seen that back home, so cool!" She tugged on her boyfriend's hand. "There's a goat! Can you believe this! So close we can touch him, but I don't know if he will snap at my hand." She opted for a photo only. "Let's just throw him a twig. Now he's munching on that thing!"

"See Tiger, looks like they just started, bet they won't be here too long 'cause they have things to do back home, 'obligations' they call it." Stella looked up as they approached.

"Hi, is there someone who can help us? We'd like to book a room." The young man held the top loop of his girlfriend's backpack as she slipped out from the straps.

Stella smiled. It wasn't unusual for people to ask for adults. "I can help you."

"Really? You look awfully young. What are you, eleven, twelve?" He placed the pack near the stone steps.

Stella laughed. "Actually, I'm only seven. I'm tall for my age. But yes, I can help you. Would you like a room? We have one available for tonight with a little terrace and you can walk out straight into the garden."

"That would be lovely, we'll take it!" The girl's eyes sparkled.

"Alright, let me see your passports and pilgrims' credentials." She rolled the guesthouse stamp in the ink on the pad and the outline of her chubby cat appeared in both credentials. She signed the date under it and handed it over to the young couple.

"What a cute stamp! Is that your cat?" The girl glanced at the doorway.

"Yes, that fluffy goodness is our Tiger. My brothers and I came up with the idea, it's for good luck along the Way. He will probably come to your window to say hello. Come, your room is ready, and you can relax."

"What a relief it will be to spend the afternoon without the backpacks." The young man rolled his shoulders up and down.

"If the packs are too much for you, we can arrange to forward them to your next place tomorrow. The other day, we had a guest and her back was bothering her, so she decided to take a break from it for a few days."

"Good to know we have this option, just in case." The girl stretched her arms above her head and bent side to side.

PILGRIM TALK   2

Thank goodness Stella's room was in the attic and not on the same level as the room where the pilgrims slept. Some of them got up way too early! She loved her room, so cozy with a nice comfy bench under a dormer window. She could pass countless hours engrossed in some book, occasionally looking up at the solid wooden beams supporting the vaulted ceiling. Not to mention the window opened up onto the flat section of the roof! She could climb out easily and crawl up pretty close to the courtyard without being detected. The pilgrims usually ate late dinner outside and shared stories of their adventures over Mama's delicious homemade dishes. Those stories brought live entertainment directly to her small village from the farthest corners of the world, by people of the world.

Stella imagined friendly love emanating from the courtyard. It struck her how complete strangers came together under one roof for the night, related their precious experiences and became the best of friends after one evening. Everyone gathered for dinner after tending to their daily chores. The pilgrims' laundry hung to dry on the clothesline outside. Colorful t-shirts, socks and shorts fluttered in the wind like a local rainbow of pilgrim colors stretching across the yard.

A bearded man with an Australian accent chatted with a fellow who relaxed in a chair and put his feet up on a stone wall. "You know, it's so liberating to have all your possessions with you in a pack. Only the essentials. I carry everything in my pack every day, all day long."

"I totally get it! I left even more of my stuff at the last place, as a donation to those in need." The man stretched out in his chair. "Initially, I struggled under the weight of my pack but gained a new fresh pace after realizing how little I needed."

Some talked about the *meseta*, the plains in the middle of Spain, as a challenge with its flat monochrome landscape and never-ending fields of wheat. "It's just you and the road… the thoughts in your head as you trudge on." A middle-aged man savored the crust of a piece of bread. "The mind couldn't find much distraction to concentrate on in the nature around me. I really had to deal with all that internal stuff that came up. Very gut wrenching, even though the walking was easy." He crossed his hands on his belly. "I did get some relief after the rain sprinkled and brought up that fresh earthy smell from the fields," he said to a woman in her thirties with a colorful bandana covering her hair. She probably spent lots of time back home making the unruly thick curls fall just the way she wanted before she faced the world each day.

"How interesting… I had such a different experience on the *meseta*." The woman twisted one curl around her finger. "Whenever I came across a green field that had bright red poppies peeking up from the ripening grain strands, it made me smile. The poppies were sprinkled all over, sometimes many together, sometimes just a few along the edge where the fields met the road. One time, the poppies took over the entire hillside, in bright red ripples, as far as I could see! They really gave me that small burst of cheer and energy I needed to get to the next town." A gentle smile appeared on her lips.

"How I enjoyed walking near fields of golden sunflowers… They bobbed their heads in the wind as if saying hello!" She grew animated and her eyes brightened. "My Spanish is not very good, but a girl mentioned that sunflower is called *girasol* which means turning with the sun." She tilted her head from side to side. "It sounded so beautiful and inspiring to me. And there was one sunflower missing some of its seeds in a pattern made to look like a smiley face, probably another pilgrim did it." She adjusted her bandana.

"It's so true what you noticed. The nature has so many ways to inspire us and support us when we need it most," a lady with an Irish accent chimed in. "Last week everyone at one hostel caught a cold. I was trying to wash my hands and do everything to avoid it." She brushed her hand over her nose. "When I started walking early that morning, my throat was feeling scratchy, and I was sneezing. A cold was about to get me too. Just then, I came to a small clearing in the forest with an abandoned house and an orchard in disarray. What did I see but a large lemon tree right by the path, heavy with large, ripe, bright yellow lemons! I picked a couple and squeezed the juice right into my water bottle. It was way too sour." She puckered her lips and scrunched up her face. "But who can complain about freshly made vitamin C! Imagine, I didn't get sick with a cold!"

"That's amazing!" A woman with curly hair held a palm to her cheek.

"The locals are super friendly here too!" Folks around the table nodded. The boyfriend from the couple Stella checked into the guesthouse earlier joined the conversation. "We got help today without even asking. We came to a fork in the road and were not sure which way to continue." His hands came together and spread apart. "Ginny and I discussed what to do when we heard someone calling "Hola! Hola!" It was a lady in the nearby house who saw us from her second-story window. She directed us emphatically and called out "Buen Camino *peregrinos*!" We learned today it means "Have a good walk, pilgrims!"

Stella heard too many wonderful stories to recount, many of them sounded almost like fairytales. Even though she couldn't put her finger on *the Camino magic*, she knew in her heart the stories were true. When most of the folks went to sleep, Stella crawled back into her room. Tiger went off on his nightly hunt to do whatever that cat did at night, which was probably not sleeping since he always loved to nap in the afternoon in the shade. As soon as Stella's head hit the pillow, she caught a whiff of the minty aroma of dried spearmint, lavender and hops her Mama sewed in a small pouch. Stella kept it under her pillow for lovely and enjoyable dreams. And how adventurous those dreams were: mountains, streams and forests in her homeland of Spain and far away corners of the world she heard about from the pilgrims.

One night she dreamt of being on a Viking ship making a journey from Norway to Spain over treacherous seas. After the group arrived on the shore, they walked on foot to Santiago. The vision was probably related to the story her parents told her recently about their friend, Anne. Stella's family wandered the streets of Oslo, Norway on vacation. Stella was still a toddler then. Her brother was on a mission to find an ice-cream shop.

"Look! There's a yellow arrow on that building." Philip pointed to a header above a doorway across the street. "Just like the arrows used to mark the way on the Camino… What are they doing in the center of Oslo?"

"From what I can make out on the sign in Norwegian, it's a pilgrims' office." Dad crossed the street for a better look. He pushed on the door and it swung open.

"Welcome! Would you like some tea and cookies? I'm Anne, by the way. Please come in, sit. Enjoy." She placed a large platter of grapes and cookies in front of them. "You can leave your backpacks here, while you explore the city if you want."

"Well, a few months later that summer, we went on the Camino in Portugal with grandma and Stella." Mama brushed Stella's hair. "We just finished visiting an old-town protected with high, star-shaped fortress walls. We were going out through its massive outside gate. Who do we see on the dusty cobblestone path? It was Anne!"

"Must be Camino magic!" Artur clapped his hands.

"Anne couldn't believe the chance meeting either! She told us that her friends finished building a replica of a Viking ship. We were all invited to come along on the ship. Then everyone could walk the Camino together on foot all the way to Santiago, just like in the old days." Mama looked out the window into the garden.

"Can we go? Can we go?" Stella and Artur jumped up and down, anticipating the adventure. Tiger just flopped the very tip of his tail up and down a few times. The most excitement you could get out of this poised creature.

"One day we will go kids! We promise!" Mama and Papa huddled over a calendar.

Tiger 3

The story of Tiger was a mystery, too. No one knew how old he was. Philip told Stella how he met the cat. "We were looking for a pet cat in the animal shelter. We passed so many different rooms with big glass windows and watched the cats inside. Some felines walked around the room like they were looking for something. Others slept curled up on soft mats. A few licked their paws and groomed themselves. They were all cute, but how do you pick if none seem to care about you being there? Somehow, after looking in several rooms, I had a feeling of someone following me." Philip lowered his voice. "I couldn't put my finger on it. Then, in the far corner of the room, I spotted two big green eyes locked on me, watching my every move."

"Really?! Was it creepy?" Stella's eyes widened.

"Until I understood what was happening… A huge, long-haired cat tracked me discretely without blinking. He was curled up on a mat and raised his head just so." Philip raised his elbow to his eye level and peeked out. "His ears tuned to my movements too, like a true hunter's."

"Wow! He was checking you out!" Stella leaned forward and covered her mouth.

"I asked the attendant to meet this curious cat. They brought him to a small room to play with us, but he was too afraid and hid under a chair. I knew he was the one." Philip's jaw relaxed. "They weighed him at 15 pounds! He seemed even larger with his long hair puffed up in a cardboard box on the way home."

"How did you pick his name?" Stella nearly tipped over her chair leaning forward.

"Because he had black stripes on his back, a white chin and a white patch on his chest, I named him Tiger." Philip grinned.

"So glad he found you, Philip! We just love this furball so!" Stella hugged Tiger who slept peacefully on her lap.

Of course, that was a long time ago. Philip went away to university and Tiger became Stella's and Artur's companion. Funny how this usually loud kitty sat perfectly quiet with her on the roof in the evenings. It's like they had their own language and understanding. It wasn't the time to attract attention to a shadowy figure of a curious little girl who should be in her comfy bed instead of climbing around on the roof. Luckily, the exhausted pilgrims didn't stay up too late after their long walk or she would have stayed there all night. Folks needed to get on the road again in the morning after breakfast. Some even left before sunrise with a headlamp, wanting to get an early start and avoid hot afternoon sun.

"How did you like your journey so far?" Stella asked an older woman, Agnes, as she adjusted her backpack straps before heading out late one morning, after most of the pilgrims already left. "Oh, it's difficult for me. My old legs can't do what they used to." Agnes bent down and rubbed her legs. "Hiking up in the mountains over the Pyrenees was exhausting. That's one of the highest points on the Camino, you know."

Stella knew she wouldn't have any trouble climbing. She smiled as Agnes went on. "I barely stumbled to the top. There was a farmer waiting for me with juicy oranges, water, and bandages for my feet. He told me he walked the Camino one time himself and knew how rewarding it was, but also how tough. Now, whenever he took a break, he waited under a large shady tree with treats to cheer up the pilgrims. You can't imagine how thankful I was to see him."

Stella nodded again.

"Ah, but you're young you wouldn't have those problems. Don't wait until you're old like me to make the pilgrimage!" Agnes stretched and rubbed her back.

"Oh, I don't plan to! I'm going to go as soon as my parents allow it." Stella stood up straighter and raised her chin.

While she was wishing Buen Camino to Agnes, the postman with a fat leather bag walked by to drop off mail. A postcard from Philip! Of course, he could have called, but that wasn't Philip. Besides, Stella loved the postcards from places he visited on breaks from school. This time it was the Grand Canyon in the US. What a breathtakingly deep and wide canyon. The postcard showed the setting sun lighting up rock formations and cliffs. A winding narrow strip of the river reflected the warm colors of the sky.

"The canyon is over a mile deep and the Colorado River slowly eroded its way in the rock over many millions of years and created this canyon. The picture doesn't do it justice. I hope someday you guys can see it in person." Stella read the card aloud.

Pretty impressive! So deep… Stella wondered how long it would take to hike down from the rim to the river. "My summer vacation is coming up, and I'll bring lots more pictures to show. Miss you all. Waiting to see you. Give Tiger a squeeze. Cheers, Philip." Stella skipped to tell her parents the news; Artur was nowhere to be seen. She ran to the stable. Tiago ate grass outside in the corral.

"Tiago! Tiago! Philip is coming soon! He can take you out to trot around. You may look all calm now, sniffing my hair, but when Philip shows up, you will be prancing!" Stella brandished the postcard. She stretched out her hand to give Tiago an apple. The horse took it gently with his warm, wet lips. He was a small horse but still huge compared to Stella. She led him close to a wooden bench nearby and stepped on the bench. From there, she stretched to the old barrel and got onto the horse.

"Let's go see my friend Alejandro, in the next village. I could walk, but this way you can stretch your legs. You know this trip with you actually takes longer than walking." She directed her horse gently. "Tiago, you stop so often to snatch that fresh grass from the side of the road. You act like you're starving! Good thing you're not a racehorse, or you wouldn't even make it to the race. It'd be over and you'd still be eating grass outside." Stella patted his neck and combed his mane with her fingers.

Long Journey Ahead 4

"There he is. I can hear him!" Stella rode up the hill. As usual, Alejandro relaxed under a shade of a large tree. He played a wooden flute while he kept an eye on a few of his family's sheep and goats that roamed the hillside nearby. His fingers fluttered over the flute openings and the sounds of the simple tune floated gracefully all around him. Stella and Tiago slowed their steps half-way up the hill not wanting to break the magic of the resonating tune. Alejandro winked as he put his breath to work on the last few notes. He waved for Stella to come up and placed the flute in his lap.

"Did you come up with a new melody? It was so gentle and light." Stella slid to the ground.

"Yeah, I improvised a little. The sheep seem to like it." He leaned over and hugged Stella.

"Those sheep are so smart, maybe that's not even a joke. We just got a postcard from Philip - from the Grand Canyon!" Stella flaunted the card near his face.

"Wow, this place looks amazing! So huge!" He ran his finger over the winding river.

"He saw it for himself, he's coming here soon!" Not soon enough in her opinion.

"That's cool! Hope he brings his guitar and we can jam a little." Alejandro tapped his fingers up and down the flute. "Hopefully we can play "House of the Rising Sun" together if he strums the cords. I've been practicing the flute score for it." He held up his flute.

"Whatever you guys choose to play is fine by me! I'll find a way to dance to it!" Stella stood and spun around on one foot and her butterfly dress twirled all around, settling just below the scrape on the knee. From climbing the apple tree probably. "Is your Grandpa home? He always has amazing stories."

"Sure, let's go find him!" Alejandro threw a quick glance at Tiago and the sheep at the bottom of the hill. "These guys know their way around, they'll be fine."

"Come on, I'll race you." Stella took off leaving her friend behind.

Nearly rolling down the hill, they almost bumped into Grandpa outside his woodworking shed. He turned around, squinting at the sun.

"I was wondering what all the commotion was, but it's just you two, my little troublemakers." He opened his arms as the children rushed in for a hug.

"Philip will be arriving from the university soon. He will stay for the summer!" Stella jumped around. "Tiago and the sheep are enjoying stuffing themselves, and we are kind of bored…" She looked at Grandpa and fluttered her eyelashes. "Please tell us another story to pass the time. Something cool and adventurous, about magic and fairy tales!"

"Hmmm." He stroked his beard. "Here's a story that has been told around this land for many centuries."

"Which one? Which one?" The friends cozied up next to him on a bench, enjoying the warm sunny day.

"It's about Santiago or Saint James. He was a pure soul, teaching here in the Iberian Peninsula about the Way to live. Though he didn't get many followers at the time. He eventually returned to Jerusalem and was killed there."

"Oh no!" Tears welled up in Stella's eyes.

"His friends were very grief-stricken but wanted to return his body to the land that was close to his heart and where he spent a lot of time teaching the Way." Grandpa gazed out into the hills.

"That's so sad! How did they manage to get here all the way from Jerusalem?" Stella considered how many months that journey would take. That's an incredible distance to cross, especially back in those days!

"There are many mysteries about what happened to Santiago's body. One of the legends is that his friends placed it in the rudderless stone boat without any sails. Somehow, with divine guidance, it made its long way across the Mediterranean Sea and up the coast of Portugal and Spain. Through the inlet and the tributary of Rio de Arousa, the boat arrived in modern-day Padron in the region of Galicia in Spain." Grandpa sighed. "Santiago was finally placed to rest somewhere on the land he loved."

"What a miraculous journey!" Alejandro stood up and paced around.

"That's not all the miracles! One day, many centuries ago a hermit noticed a star in the sky pointing to a specific place in a field in Galicia." Grandpa stretched his hand up and drew a line with his finger all the way to the ground. "The man felt the place must be special, so he called the bishop to investigate. That location was determined to be Santiago's resting place. Since then, the place has been called Santiago de Compostela, Santiago of the field of stars. A beautiful cathedral honors this magical place. Many have journeyed by foot to pay their respects to Santiago."

"That's where the Camino leads!" Now Stella jumped up. "I so want to go but my parents say I am too young! They can't leave the guesthouse during the busy season." She lowered her head and pouted.

"You are very young but very spirited. Don't worry, the time will come." He stroked her head. "This reminds me of a very important letter for someone in Santiago, but I can't go there myself now either. Don't know if it will be safe if delivered by mail…"

"Why is this letter so important, Grandpa?" Alejandro stared at his grandfather.

"Well, if I told you, it wouldn't be a secret mission, would it?" Grandpa winked.

"No, guess not…" Alejandro focused on his shoes and kicked the dirt.

"But, maybe if…" He tapped his finger on his lip. "If you can convince Philip to go with you…" A note of conspiracy popped up in his voice. "I bet your parents would give permission if Philip came along…" Stella perked up and looked at him sideways. "But can I trust you, a bunch of hooligans, to deliver it to Santiago?" Grandpa raised an eyebrow and scratched the back of his head.

Stella and Alejandro exchanged a look, their signal from years of small mischief together. "Yes! you can," they said in unison. "We won't get caught or spill the beans!" Stella's eyes darted from her friend to his grandfather.

"In a way it's perfect, nobody will think twice to question little kids…" Grandpa lowered his voice and motioned them to come closer. Not like the sheep would hear it… "Listen, there is a nun, Sister Maria, who volunteers in the pilgrims' office… You would get a huge reward if you can deliver the letter safely."

"I don't care about the reward! I just want to go!" Stella bounced from one foot to the other. "Can we take Tiago with us? Would it be suspicious?" She glanced over her shoulder.

"We so love this horse!" Alejandro looked at Tiago on the hill, still munching grass and swatting flies with his tail.

"You will need his help." Grandpa admired Tiago's sturdy muscular build.

"So, it is settled then!" A tiny smirk rolled over Stella's lips as she pondered the mission. "Not a peep about the letter, we are just young pilgrims on the way to Santiago."

"If Philip and your parents agree that is…" Alejandro lifted up his chin.

"I'll take care of it, don't you worry." Stella's little hands rested on her bony hips, and she kicked a small stone with her bare foot.

The time until Philip's arrival seemed to drag on forever. But then one morning Stella spotted him from way far down the street, walking from the train station with a guitar case on his back and small school backpack in this hand.

"Artur! I see Philip!" She ran towards her big brother, skillfully avoiding the pilgrims on the trail. Stella closed in on him laughing and not slowing down, aiming for his belly with her head. Philip dropped his backpack and managed to grab her under the arms, just milliseconds before the pretend collision. Big brother and his feather-light sister spun around giggling, the same way they'd done a million times before, ever since she was a tiny toddler. Seconds later, Artur jumped in for a bear hug.

"I can carry your backpack to the house." Artur delivered it to the doorstep with care the world's greatest treasure would require.

"Our boy knows how to pack light!" Papa patted his oldest on the back. Philip had matured so much over the school year.

"Since the time I had to carry my own pack on the Camino, nothing but the essentials for every trip! Even managed to fit in the gifts for you guys from the Grand Canyon." Philip had to bend down to kiss mom on the cheek.

Stella gave Philip some time and space to settle in but kept her Camino plan fresh in her head. It took some time, but not much work, to convince both sets of parents, though the chances with the big brother were 50/50. It won't be a slam dunk. Why he would want to take a group of younglings in his care all the way to Santiago? One morning, as he was still a bit groggy from jetlag, Stella scooted over next to him on a terrace with a bowl of green pea pods.

"I picked these for you from the garden. You arrived just in time. Artur almost got to them, like he chomps down everything else. I convinced him to leave at least the peas for his big brother!"

"Yummy! Thanks, sis!" Philip crunched on a pod. "Mom and I used to call these our addiction. Whenever we got a bag from the supermarket, we couldn't stop eating until the whole bag of these crunchies was gone!" He picked three more with the other hand.

"I heard! Mama had a few pods but saved the best for you." She slid the bowl across the table closer to Philip and watched her brother.

"Sweet! What have you been up to?" He snapped a pod open, pushed the peas out with his thumb and smacked his lips. "What's your newest scheme with Artur? Where is that boy all the time anyway?"

"Well… We have a little secret, it's not a big deal… but…" Stella pushed her thumbnail into the soft wood of the table.

"Am I kid enough to know what it is?" Philip sucked in the peas one by one.

"Kinda… and grown enough that the adults would trust you." Stella finished the heart imprint with her fingernail on the table.

"What kind of trouble are you in, my little princess?" Philip pushed a strand of Stella's hair from her face.

"It's no trouble, really, it's super-secret though. Can you promise you won't tell?" She stared directly at him.

"No, I won't promise any such thing! If you're about to set the house on fire with your pyrotechnic experiments, I will tell for sure!" He plopped the empty bowl on the table.

"It's nothing like that!" Stella sucked the air in. "Alejandro's Grandpa has a special letter to deliver to a nun in Santiago. He trusts us, the kids, enough to deliver it, that's all."

"No way am I walking the whole Way to Santiago from here! And with you three monkeys!" Philip pushed himself away from the table.

"All right, fine! No biggie. We can just stay here and finish building the shed that Papa needs for his tools. He's been raving about it and how excited he is that you are coming! To have the special manly bonding time with you while building that thing. First to plan it out, then to pick just the right materials, to pour the foundation…"

"Girl, you know dad way too well! He's going to be working on that thing day and night until it is just perfect, it could take the whole summer!" Philip got up and paced around the table.

"Maybe... You don't want to build a shed with Papa? Is it true that he shut down the Wi-Fi before to get you to do stuff besides playing on the computer?" Stella crossed her fingers behind her back.

"Darn it! Going to Santiago sure beats building a shed..." He kicked a tiny dust pile.

"You are the best big brother ever!" Stella flung her arms around her brother's neck and gave him a peck on the cheek. "When do you want to leave?"

"When is dad planning to get started on that shed?" Philip untangled her arms and laughed.

After a few days of planning the essentials for the pilgrim journey, they were ready to follow the Camino's yellow arrows through their village towards Santiago de Compostela. Philip took charge of the special letter, stuffed it deep in the inner pocket of his fleece. It's been a joke in the family he would enjoy the Camino more if he could ride a horse. He got his wish after so many years. Philip rode atop Tiago, holding the reins with one hand and guarding his younger brother with the other in a saddle in front of him. Stella and Alejandro followed on foot with little backpacks full of snacks and extra change of clothes. They stuffed in their jackets in case it got cooler in the evenings. Her sneakers stayed in the backpack too as she enjoyed the warm cobblestones underfoot.

"Please take this flashlight with you, just in case you are out after dark." Grandpa patted Alejandro on the back.

"Mom, looks like Tiger is coming with us too!" Artur waited for Tiger trotting behind them, waving his fluffy tail.

"Ok, Buen Camino! Be safe! Give me a few extra hugs before you take off." Mama squeezed Stella, then Alejandro, and touched the boys' feet dangling from the horse.

"They will be fine, honey, don't worry." Papa put his hand around her shoulders as they waved from the doorstep of the guesthouse.

"To Santiago!" Artur proudly declared and motioned forward.

As they walked out of the village, the neighbors cracked their windows and waved. "Buen Camino peregrinos!" sounded from all directions as everyone wished them good luck on the Way.

The motivated group walked farther and farther out of the familiar territory. The locals recognized them as pilgrims on the Way to Santiago by the seashell Grandfather attached to Tiago's saddlebag. The shell became the symbol of the Camino over the centuries. Many folks wished them Buen Camino! and followed the young pilgrims down the road with amazed and amused glances.

Philip, the Camino veteran, educated the first-timers. "The Way is marked by the yellow arrows pointing in the correct direction. We should be able to find the arrows carefully painted any place where one would question which way to turn. There are also stone markers placed along the Way. They show a yellow shell on a blue background at the top part of the marker, number of kilometers remaining till Santiago, and yellow arrow pointing which way to go. See this marker, a long way is still remaining."

"Well, we just started. Let's just skip them, the stone markers. If we don't look at the distances on them this far out, it will be easier." Stella thought her proposal was brilliant.

"Why do you care about the distance anyway, Philip?" Alejandro looked up cheekily. "You're riding a horse on the Camino, just like you always wanted. You may need to take Tiger up there with you too if he gets tired."

Artur giggled. "That's the funniest statement ever!" As he burst out in his contagious laugh, nobody could contain theirs.

They rolled along trading jokes through a few villages. A welcoming stone church seemed to call them from around the bend in the road. The priest tugged on his black robe up as he stepped over a high door jam, pulled the door shut and fumbled for the keys. He saw the shell on their saddlebag and wished them a Buen Camino! He asked if they wanted stamps in their pilgrims' passports.

"We didn't have a chance to pick them up yet. Do you have any?" Philip climbed down from the horse.

"Yes, certainly. Don't forget to put two stamps each day as you start walking on your last 100 km into Santiago. You can put more in each location you pass to remember the places later. Present your passports in the pilgrims' office to receive a Compostela, a certificate of completion for those who walk the Camino for religious or spiritual purposes."

"That last 100 km seems so far away for now, but we will make it there in no time. Right?" Philip smacked a high five on Alejandro's palm.

Alejandro and Stella followed the priest inside the cool stone church where he placed the first ink stamp into each booklet. They wrote their names in each credential and examined the ink imprints of the church.

"Buen Camino, peregrinos! Keep these in a safe place so they don't get wet if it rains." The priest locked the church door.

"Gracias!" The refreshed group waved in unison and got on their way after filling their water bottles at the fountain outside. Soon they added another level to their game of not noticing the stone markers.

"Do you see a stone?" Alejandro pointed his finger.

"What stone?" Stella raised her shoulders.

"There is a stone right there!" Artur moved to the side of the path.

"Ok, I will just skip it." Stella laughed and hopped on one foot.

Bursting with laughter, they advanced. Then the competition started – who would see the next yellow arrow first. Usually, Stella or Alejandro spotted them first. But then Artur saw the next arrow from way up high on the horse.

"There! There! We need to turn now." He bounced in the saddle and pointed his index finger.

Philip gladly observed all this. "At least you're keeping yourselves entertained, could be worse if you munchkins got bored. Tiger will have to entertain you when you run out of tricks." Tiger purred in his lap. "Good to see you, pal, nothing phases you. I missed your furry tail." Philip squeezed the cat tightly, his pet and friend even before his sister and brother were born.

COBBLESTONE PATH   5

"Can we take a break, guys? It's getting a little hot." Alejandro brushed a drop of sweat from his forehead and flicked it off.

"Let's head over to the shade of that sycamore tree. We are doing great for the first day!" Philip lowered Artur from the saddle and stretched his legs. "Alejandro, take your sneakers off to give your feet some air so you don't get blisters. How are your feet, Stella? You don't want to put your sneakers on?"

"Not yet, I'm fine." Stella wiggled her dusty toes. "These ancient cobblestones are tough though." Most of the stones were still intact and shone in spots from years of wear. A few moved out of alignment along the edges of the path. Pretty impressive still, considering how long ago they were laid. Some stones were in disarray and turned on their sides a little farther up the hill, probably due to a rush of water or a mudslide. Stella picked a smooth wide rock and set her backpack down. She leaned into the tall grass sprinkled with tiny white and yellow wildflowers, resting her back on the hillside. "Aaaahhh. So nice." She exhaled. "We earned this rest."

"You know, some sections we walked on today are part of the preserved old Roman road that went across Spain and passed the town of Astorga." Philip passed the bottle of water to everyone and poured a little in his hand for Tiger. "As Tiago's hoofs stomped on the road, I felt like a Roman soldier and imagined the chariots rushing by. Some carried the warriors, some heavy carts loaded with provisions and goods of their times." He brandished a pretend sword. "That's the beauty of living history, of going back in time on this journey."

"I can picture it." Alejandro closed his eyes. "Since the old times, many walked on this road either in their daily duties or on a pilgrimage, looking for something. It's like I feel the presence of those ancient pilgrims. Their footsteps gently touched this earth as they left their homes, their daily lives in search of their spiritual truths."

"Kinda like we did. Finally, it all came together so we could go on the Camino! Can you believe that we are here?!" Stella nudged Artur. "The ground is pretty warm today; no wonder, 'cos it's so hot outside." She examined the bottoms of her feet.

"That's true. The pilgrims of old had something in common, they all heard a call in their hearts, a clear call, no mistakes about it. Some probably heard it in the morning at sunrise while tending to their livestock. Some felt it as a sharp pang in the chest on the way to the shop or the bakery. Some heard the whisper in their ear to set out on the way to Santiago. To walk the Way from their home with an open heart and clear spirits. To listen to messages that presented to them along the way." Philip patted Stella on her shoulder. "The path called you as it called many others before. I am proud of you, little sis, that you recognized it too." She scrunched her nose and smiled.

"Is the letter safe? You still got it?" Alejandro felt the pocket of Philip's jacket.

"Are these cobblestones magical?" Artur chewed on a blade of grass. "Do they have some hidden magnetism to appeal to each person precisely at the right time? Are the ancient footsteps unseen but heard by the internal mechanisms of the body? Is the ground itself transmitting the message like a telephone?" Stella's jaw dropped as she looked Artur up and down. "Did I say something wrong?" Artur blushed.

She shook her head no. "You are awfully young to… But then I get that a lot too. Just be you. You're doing great."

"Is that the magic of the path when many were called to it but couldn't explain the calling?" Alejandro threw a few breadcrumbs to a tiny chickadee that swooshed down from the nearby beech tree. The bird observed the resting pilgrims for a while and finally got close to them. It watched the crumbs from a safe distance. They admired its white chest and gentle yellow sides contrasting with gray wings and much darker head. Everyone sat very still. Artur held Tiger back and stroked behind his ears. Finally, the bird got enough courage and dashed for the crumbs. He left in a flash with his winnings. Alejandro chuckled and scooted closer to Philip.

"Maybe it's not important to know why the magic works but just to trust it once it made itself known." Philip tapped his hand on his heart. "To trust the inner voice for taking a break, for setting time aside for the quest to clear the mind, to look and listen to higher connections." *They still seem to be paying attention, let me continue.* "In the noise and fog of the rushing about our responsibilities and activities, we can often set aside that gentle calling as non-essential. Other matters become more pressing and take priority. All the magical methods of the Way make themselves known to attract our attention." He looked at everyone. Impressive that they listened that far. Hopefully, he'd have some other pearls of wisdom if they wanted to hear more.

"From the pilgrims' stories I heard at the guesthouse… some saw it as the bright colors of the rainbow, some felt it in the cool moisture of the morning fog. Some believed they heard it in a bird song." Stella left out that she heard the stories from the rooftop. "Many people faced turbulent times before they could arrange everything and get on the Way." Another bird chirped somewhere nearby.

"Turbulence before the journey leads to peace as people process various emotions and deal with their feelings." Philip remembered the times he followed his parents on the Camino. "All kinds of stuff came up before our trips to Santiago with mom and dad."

Alejandro rubbed his chin. "Is the magic of the Camino to turn challenges into blessings through learning? Is the magic to remove the superficial from the mind one step at a time as the feet touch the freedom of the open way?"

I've been away for less than a year, Philip thought. *What do these children do all day to come up with all these insights? This is going to be an interesting trip, so long as no one gets hurt or loses an eye.*

Lost in the Forest

6

Just like that, Tiago was gone. He was eating grass on the side of the trail while they rested. Then boom! As if someone snapped his fingers, he wasn't there. They didn't hear him stomping off, not that he would do that anyway.

"Guys, where's Tiago?" Stella looked around frantically. No trace of the missing horse, no crumpled grass beyond where he stood eating, no broken branches. No plants missing their flowers. Nothing but the woods beyond. Giant pine trees stood guard as if daring them to enter.

"He is right there, what do you mean?" Philip pushed himself up, noticing a worried undertone in Stella's question.

"No, he's gone!" Her little fists tightened and turned white. "You know I don't worry for nothing, but I don't have a good feeling about this."

"He has never done that before." Alejandro moved aside a floppy pine branch for a better look.

"How is this possible, it's like he evaporated." Artur put down his sandwich.

"Tiger, did you see him?" Philip ran his hand down Tiger's tail. The cat lifted his ear, he was taking a nap and didn't see anything, obviously. But it was worth a question since they were desperate.

"Gotta go look for him." Artur stuffed the last piece of sandwich in his mouth and swallowed barely chewing it.

"We lost a horse… How can you lose a horse that was there just a second ago?" Philip picked up his jacket and stuffed it into his pack, running different scenarios in his head. "This situation could turn dire quickly. Well, technically the time reference doesn't matter since time is relative."

"That's why they say 'time flies when you are having fun' or 'I have been waiting for an eternity.'" Alejandro lifted his chin and pulled his shoulders back.

"Great observation." Philip exhaled the words through his teeth and sealed his lips. Great time to be learning about time relativity. "Though, we are still missing our horse! Let's pack up our snacks and head out that way since no one has seen him cross the trail. Just keep track of where we go. We'll need to get back to the trail eventually."

"Guys, we called and walked for hours, but no sign of Tiago." Artur climbed up on a natural rock pile for a better look.

"At least he has plenty to eat and drink here, but we're all getting very hungry. Let's head to the village and we can start looking again in the morning." Philip touched Tiger's nose sticking out from the bag on his shoulder.

"I don't want to leave Tiago here all alone." Artur slid down the rocks, his chin trembled just slightly. "He is my buddy, what if he's scared?"

"Artur is right." Stella got a little closer to Philip. "Maybe he will turn up just before dusk."

"What if you all get scared as it gets dark soon? The forest talks at night with all these creeks and cracks and swooshes. Every chipmunk starts looking the size of racoon and every owl sounds like a pterodactyl coming to take you away to his nest at the top of a cliff." Philip shook his water bottle. *Great, almost full.* No one had touched it since the last natural spring they drank from.

"Yes, very possible, but what choice do we have? Which way is the village?" Alejandro paced and curled his arms over his head. They were in a meadow with a single knotted and twisted oak tree. No trail leading in or out. The darkening outline of the forest nearby did not look inviting.

"All right, we can stay and wait for him since I haven't heard of any bears around here. We can camp under this huge oak tree." *Feels better out here in the open. If it gets too windy, we can move to the forest, but I wouldn't rush there now.* "What do we have left for snacks? It will have to be our dinner, plus those raspberries over there. Let's gather leaves and tall grass for some cushion before it gets too dark. Be careful though." Everyone got to work but not without looking over their shoulders at the massive mysterious forest.

Philip suddenly felt energized in this element, like a commander of a tiny troop, stuffing down his fear of darkness. "I have Grandfather's flashlight here if we really need it, but let's get ready and get our eyes adjusted to the twilight around us." Nobody else spoke for a while. They gathered whatever plant material seemed somewhat soft and carried it like little working ants to their nest at the base of the ancient oak. "Luckily, it's a warm evening guys, but you may need your jackets for the night. Don't go wandering in the dark, please. Tiger, you too! Don't want to lose you to some wild animal." He pulled out the last piece of *jamon* left over from lunch and fed it to the cat in little strips.

"Then what do we do?" Artur dumped handfuls of dry leaves in a pile and pressed on it to test for softness.

"Now we sit and practice patience." Philip sat down cross-legged with his hands on his knees and thumbs touching the middle fingers forming a circle.

"Funny, very funny, Philip!" Stella pulled on her jacket and glanced towards a darkening wall of pine trees. She got chills from that direction every time. "What animals besides bears can there be? Who knows what's in this grass…" The constant rustling of the meadow inhabitants against the backdrop of the cicadas did not sound reassuring.

"Wolves…" He grinned and bared his teeth with a scowl. "I was only half-joking though about patience." He scanned his crew. All here, good. "We got nothing else to do but to trust that everything will be ok. Let's try to focus on how that feels." Stella raised an eyebrow. "But we need to create a safe space first. I'll show you how. Scoot over closer everyone, then close your eyes. Good… Imagine a transparent bubble all around you, at about arm's length."

"What kind of bubble is it?" Artur squeezed his eyelids shut and dragged his palms down his pant legs.

"Can be something like a shimmery soap bubble or a gently glowing golden sphere. Now imagine that it's filled with whatever you need in this moment – warmth, comfort, safety. Nothing dangerous can get in. Is it working for you?"

"Yeah, kinda." Stella hugged her knees to her chest.

"Just relax, imagine that it's your personal space created just for you to feel good. When you relax in it, you will feel very peaceful." Philip's breathing evened out as he kept talking.

"Ok, almost got it." Alejandro smiled and softened his grip on the zipper of his jacket.

"Think about how awesome we did so far. We always had plenty of water, food, we stayed together, got help from folks when we needed it. Think about all the little things that have gone right so far." Philip turned his hands palms up.

"Yeah, that's true! That sweet lady in a village who greeted us with a plate of crepes. So tasty! And the sugar she sprinkled on them – yum!" Stella was licking her lips as her jaw relaxed.

"See how those positive experiences and thoughts can carry us even in this tough time." Philip discerned a distant hoot of an owl.

"You're right! I thought it would be pretty scary to be in the forest at night." Alejandro moved a bit closer to Stella and Artur.

As if he didn't know, Philip straightened his back. "It can be, but fear creeps in only if you think something can go wrong. If you know you are exactly in the right place, at exactly the right time, everything will be exactly as it should be. Fear has no place in your heart because you are so sure that the challenges will bring amazing rewards." Where was all this coming from? Was the forest speaking through him? "Try to spin fear into gold and see what happens."

"How?" Artur crossed his legs and moved a few leaves from one pile to another, sorting them by shape and size.

"Let's say fear hides somewhere in the pit of your stomach. Every time you discover an unfamiliar situation or decide to try something new, you go to unknown territory without previous guidance. If you let fear get heavy and take over, you wouldn't move a step." Philip clutched his stomach.

"I would still be sitting on my front porch at home all alone?" Alejandro cringed.

"Now imagine a ball of golden yarn in a basket at home with that golden string attached to your stomach. For every step you take into the unknown, you need to spin that fear into a longer golden string to allow movement." Philip turned his head to a distant hoot of an owl. Must be out on his hunt for mice in the meadow. "You wouldn't allow fear to hold you back. In fact, you would convert it into something beneficial instead. The farther you go, the more fear you spin into the golden string of confidence, experience and knowledge, the bigger the benefits of your journey would be growing in your heart and mind."

"And there would be nothing left from that fear." Artur rocked back and forth. Philip smiled at his companions as they became a bit more animated. *Did the confidence replace fear so gently that nobody even noticed? Not gonna question it, since this kind of talk seems to be working for everyone.* He noticed a rising crescent moon casting a mystical tint on treetops. *That must be east, just above that funny shaped hill where the first star is sparkling. Stars will be out in multitudes very soon.*

"Who knows why Tiago is not here..." Alejandro moved out a branch that poked him in the leg. "Maybe he wanted to tell us that we should hang around like this sometimes, listen to the crickets under the stars, smell the lavender and sage, play with the acorns and let the wind rustle our hair. Maybe Tiago knows it's pretty safe and so should we."

"The grass smells so calming." Stella took in a breath full of the aroma as she struggled to keep her eyes open and her head on the backpack, the world's most uncomfortable pillow.

"Let's see if we can spot some shooting stars." Philip arched his back and looked up. Quiet murmuring came from Artur and Alejandro in response. Tiger was already fast asleep at their feet since he wasn't allowed to hunt with the risk of being hunted himself in the wilderness. It's possible Philip got a little too worried in the evening and a little overprotective, but he kept a lid on those feelings. Mom and dad didn't need to know about this starry night open-air adventure. Maybe the darkness wasn't the issue after all. Feeling a little disoriented without the sense of sight makes other senses stronger. So helpful that his intuition kicked in and the right words flowed in speaking to his travel mates. It was different today somehow as he put his own words into practice. Philip put his head down on the scrunched-up jacket under his head, moved the all-important letter a bit to the side and drifted off.

Waiting to be Born   7

"Good morning sleepy head!" Artur whispered to Stella as she stretched and rubbed her eyes. "Wake up! Look at the color of that morning sky!"

"Wow! Those rosy pinks and peachy oranges creeping up on the turquoise of the whole sky! Thanks for waking me up." Stella sat up on her bed of oak leaves and grass. "Last night wasn't the most comfortable sleep, but this view is totally worth it."

"Yeah, I tried to tell you before at home, but you and your beauty rest. Listen, I had the craziest dream just prior to waking up." He lowered his voice. "Want to tell you before I forget how special it was. So moving."

"Haven't heard you speak like that ever." Stella brushed her hand against the grass and drops of morning dew shimmered on her outstretched palm.

"Yes, very surreal. I had a feeling of waiting to be born ever since our family moved to Spain." Artur's eyed glowed in a way she hadn't seen before. "It was like the idea of me was present with our family for a while."

"Really? What do you mean?" Stella hugged her legs tighter and pulled her dress over her knees against the morning chill.

"I was like a whiff of white dandelion fuzz floating in the air and then hovering among the stars. From here, I chose my siblings: you, the adventurous little girl and Philip, thoughtful older brother; because you both loved spending time in nature. I could see that you both searched for the mystery in everything, for the practical secret of the beauty of our world. How it comes from the complexity combined with simplicity and creates such a beautiful planet."

"Whoa, that's deep, little brother!" Stella stared at the changing color show in the sky.

"From way up there, I looked down on glowing blue oceans, bright green forests, yellow sandy deserts, browns of fertile lands, blinding white snow of the polar icecaps… I could perceive the colors below from there, but not the sounds. The undivided silence with a gentle undertone of all-sustaining and all-inclusive love enveloped me there, in the great beyond. The love that made me curious to explore this colorful land. It made me feel comfortable and safe that all will go according to the divine plan when I chose to join this marvelous world."

"Did you see the colors and light from the stars?" Stella swallowed.

"There were no colors among the deep reaches of the sky except for deep velvety black depth. It was alive and like another expression of the light, similar to the multidimensional colors of the rainbow. The black was the inspiration to go explore bigger and deeper aspects of creation."

"This is a lot to take in…" Stella removed a dewy stone stuck to her big toe. "Maybe this forest is magical."

"That's why I wanted to tell you. I am still processing all this..." Artur rubbed his forehead. "So, I was observing the live atmosphere of the earth wondering how it would be to breathe that sweet fresh air of the forests or the cool breeze of the seaside. I saw opportunities to experience every day, when I would be ready to take them. I wondered what mom's touch would feel like when I would be born. How tasty is the milk on the lips of a newborn? How does it feel to learn to walk, to run, to sing, to read? Those answers can't be accessed from way up high. Only the choice to experience them personally in the physical life on this beautiful planet."

"How did you do it?" Stella tapped her fingers on her knee.

"I reached out to our mom through a whiff of the wind. She was playing with you on the lawn. She blew white star-shaped seeds of dandelions into the air and you chased them." He pursed his lips and blew. "The wind brought her the message that I was ready to join the family. While you ran around with yellow dandelions in your hand and a wreath in your hair, mom picked up the white one. She blew on it, from the depth of her belly, sending all the white star seeds into the air and her intention into the universe. It was then clear to me that the right time came to join my chosen family. Very soon after, I arrived to our parents as a squirmy newborn amazed by the intentionality of my choice."

"I remember your deep thoughtful eyes of the color that only newborns have. Adults don't have it. You had the eyes that knew all the mysteries but waited for the body to catch up to materialize them in this life." Stella looked at him lovingly. "With the eyes whose intention was known by everyone who held you as the newcomer to this world but couldn't explain what you meant. Now I understand, we were so far removed from where you came from, among the stars. You grew up so very quickly and soon we were running and playing in the fields of the tall green grass." She touched Artur's hand. "Thank you for sharing this dream with me. It means the world to me that you told me! Now I can finally put the words what I felt when I saw you for the first time." Stella threw her arms around her little brother.

"Now I can remember where I came from. I saw the wonders of this planet infused with the divine light and vibration of love that I first felt among the stars. Now when I look at the stars at night, I will remember that love and different manifestations it takes. No matter how far the stars may look, the bridge of love that extends out is always available for anyone..." He squeezed her fingers. "Glad I was able to share this with you, my crazy sister."

"What do you think is in that letter we are carrying?" Stella took a stick and drew a rectangle in the dust. With a triangle on top, like an envelope flap.

"I don't know." Artur put on a fresh pair of socks and slid his feet into his sneakers. "It doesn't matter."

"Aren't you the slightest bit curious?" She glanced at the corner of the envelope sticking out from Philip's jacket pocket.

"I am interested, but Grandpa sealed it for a reason." Artur frowned.

"Well, if he trusted us to carry it, he would trust us to know what's in it, right?" Stella raised her eyebrows, scrunching her forehead, and made a fake smile. "Maybe the seal is just for other people…"

"Wrong! It's sealed for everyone except Sister Maria in Santiago!" He pulled tight on his right shoelace. "So Cut It Out!"

"Didn't know you felt so strongly about it." Stella stared at the ground. "Thanks for putting me straight. Love you to the moon and back, baby brother! Let's wake up the boys so they can see the sky too. It's getting some raspberry undertones now – above the treetops there."

"When are you gonna stop calling me a baby?" Artur put both hands on his hips.

"Mama says we will always be her babies." Stella reached over to wake up Philip. "Geesh, he still sleeps like a log."

Dragonfly 8

"I see a little pond over there, let's check it out in case Tiago wanted to find a place for a drink." Everyone followed Alejandro through waist-high grass.

"What's that?" Stella grabbed Philip's arm and pulled him back. He pushed her behind him with one hand and Artur with the other. Alejandro halted in his tracks. Stella peered around his side. The dragonfly hovered just above the pond as a rock landed. Water droplets splashed on its transparent, shimmery wings.

Stella pushed Philip's hand aside and came out from behind him, drawn by the beauty and light. Philip tried to stop her. "It means no harm." She stepped forward entranced by its elegance. The dragonfly hovered over the lily ever so slightly, twirling its wings and showing off an amazing slide show as if projected by an invisible hand. The reflection of never-before-seen colors appeared in those droplets. The warm light shimmered and sparkled iridescently from the wings of the dragonfly and spread all the way to the shore. "It seems the birds should chase it, but they admire the dragonfly too." Pink waterlilies opened wider to the sun and welcomed its warmth joyfully.

"Who threw the rock? It couldn't have just rolled from anywhere with all this grass around." Philip broke the spell.

"Anyone there?" As he turned around, all of a sudden, he faced men on horseback in full body armor.

"Knights?" Artur started toward them, but Philip pulled him back.

"No, leave him," Stella said. "They won't hurt us. Look at them."

The Knights on their tall horses surrounded the kids and stared. They examined each other in wonder and amazement. Neither party moved in astonishment. The horses chewed on their ornate bridles.

"The Templars!" Philip recognized them by the famous light overcoats with a red cross under the beige mantles also with a red cross. Metal mesh headdress protected their heads and covered the necks, flowing all the way to their chests. The metal mesh tunics fell below their knees. "I heard their mission was protecting the pilgrims from robbers in the old days. Now I get it, beige probably looked white under the bright sun, causing a modern misconception!"

The men examined the young pilgrims head to toe from the height of their horses but kept their swords sheathed. They exchanged knowing and meaningful glances with each other. Tiger who broke the lengthy silence. "Meow, meow! Why are they here?" he seemed to say.

"Shoosh, Tiger!" Stella petted her flustered pet. "We will figure it out soon. Just stay close and don't wander off spooking the horses, please." Stella could only surmise how they looked to these men. She chuckled at their confused faces.

"Where do you come from with the strange clothing and footwear?" The leader spoke a throaty Spanish they were not accustomed to hearing. The cadence of his speech sounded unusual too. The inflections, word patterns and the tone of his voice vibrated with a heavy influence of Latin.

Stella glanced at her feet, at Philip, Alejandro, and Artur and laughed. Surely, they looked odd to these men with their clingy clothes and slender figures. One of the men rode his horse toward her and stopped just in front. The horse smelled the flower in her hair, snorted, and sneezed. Probably from the dust that clung to it. Artur giggled. Stella squeezed Tiago's empty bridle still in her hands. The Knights instinctively looked around for the horse. But the horse was nowhere to be seen.

"What is your meaning to be here?" The leader moved his horse a few steps closer and leaned towards Philip.

"Good day, Honorable Knights." Philip hesitated a bit, he motioned Artur behind. "We walked on the Camino trail in the plains, towards a large castle on the hill, looking for some shade and water. Our horse Tiago wandered off. We searched for him, spent the night in the forest and seem to have walked out somewhere entirely new."

"Are you part of Noches Templarios fiesta procession, the Knights Templar reenactment? We hear the holiday celebration is coming up in Ponferrada." Stella checked out the metal spurs on the men's boots at about her eye level. "Your outfits look pretty authentic. Even your accent sounds believable."

"Your statement about reenactment puzzles us. We are busy with our daily patrols and duties. There is no time for games outside of regular training." He moved his gaze back to Philip. "Those who are not in combat, have many duties including managing the construction of fortifications, running economic parts of our duties or learning philosophy and theology in the great library in the castle you mention." The man placed his hand on the mane of the horse as he spoke. "Where are you coming from and where are you going? You say you are pilgrims, but you appear rather different."

"We come from Astorga, most recently. Our last stop was at the pilgrim guesthouse at the village outside it. We are on our way to Santiago, the cathedral more specifically." Philip left out the part about their letter and the real reason for their pilgrimage.

"The inn there is run by our brothers, the one with the goose imprint on the front door." Another Knight nudged his horse forward.

"Yes, but... The keepers are very attentive to the needs of the walking pilgrims." Philip showed the Camino shell on his backpack. The leader extended his lance and skillfully drew the pack from Philip's hands by the top loop. The shell clanked against the pack buckle. Philip's jaw dropped and his hands froze as if still holding the pack in front of him. What just happened? How does he even grip the lance with that clumsy metal mesh glove? The Knight took a closer look at the pack and passed it around to others. It's like they haven't seen the shell before, or the backpack. What century are they from? Philip suppressed his laugh. "Sometimes it is hard for us to find shelter with the horse though. Have you seen him nearby? His name is Tiago, a chocolate, black color with a brown mane."

"No, we didn't see him near the pond. What do they call you?" The leader's face softened a bit.

"Philip, my sister, Stella and her friend, Alejandro. Our younger brother is Artur who acts like the king already, with his royal cat Tiger."

"Pleasure to meet you, pilgrims. My name is George. We can escort you to the castle. It is our duty to protect the pilgrims." He put his hand on his heart. "Though, I must say, you younglings are the first of this kind I've ever seen." The rest of the troop let out a laugh after this statement and the metal clanked. The horses sounded like they got the joke too and snorted.

"You are the first of this kind we've seen, too." Stella said under her breath. Alejandro snorted. She pulled on Philip's hand. "Do you think it's ok to go with them?"

"Not like we have much choice." He whispered. "He does sound genuine, but his manners are a bit antiquated."

"To say the least…" Alejandro cocked his head and stepped sideways for a better look at the men's attire.

"Climb up, younglings, let's keep an eye for Tiago as we ride." George assigned each kid to a rider.

The Knights lifted them up. Artur took the apprehensive Tiger in his arms and whispered something in his ear. The mismatched group moved on from the pond, looking like a traditional depiction of Templar Knights, with two riders on each horse.

"Look, the dragonfly is still in the same spot but the soft light emanating from its wings has dimmed." Stella watched as the dragonfly gently vanished. "Who knows where or when?"

"To another time or another dimension maybe. I had a strange premonition earlier about the day turning out extraordinary." George rubbed his beard.

"Why did you throw the rock in the pond?" Stella got to ride with George.

"We don't know who threw the rock. When it fell in the pond this morning, it crossed two worlds and created ripples on the surface in time." He kept his gaze on the path. "The disturbance was tangible on all levels. Even the waterlilies' stringy roots clinging to a rock and the fish felt it all the way at the bottom of the pond. The fish sensed the unusual vibration and paused for a second. If there is such a thing as a second. You asked for the explanation of something very profound, little girl."

"Then you guys showed up." Stella had a smirk on her face.

"It's what they call a ripple in time. Even the ancients had stories about it, but no one knows for sure how it works. As the circular vibrations in the water materialized, they became the physical image of the rift."

"The forest last night was magical too!" Artur overheard the conversation.

"Everything is possible, we just don't know our abilities." Artur's companion Knight kept his horse lined up behind the leader.

"How do you guys know all this? Aren't you here to just to protect the pilgrims?" Artur turned back to his rider.

"We have many purposes in this land, some more apparent than others," said the Knight as he gave their horse a touch of the spurs.

Arriving at the Temple 9

"Would you like to spend the night here in our castle?" George extended the offer of Templar hospitality. "We're not sure where you come from, but it's not really safe to sleep out in the forest these days."

"We can stay in a real castle?! With real Knights?" Artur jumped up and down in the saddle. "Did you hear that, Philip?"

"Yes, of course! We would, thank you!" Philip managed to get the words out after he caught his breath.

"How cool is this?!" Stella turned to see her brothers, still amazed and hardly believing the turn of events. We are riding real battle horses in full gear with ribbons across the front of their chests.

"Just like in the old books!" Alejandro petted the mane of his warhorse.

The group crossed the sturdy bridge made of wrought iron and wooden beams spanning over the Rio Sil. George motioned to the astounded guards to grant passage.

"Ponferrada means iron bridge!" Alejandro almost fell off his horse. The name of the town is Ponferrada, the iron bridge! Now I get it!"

Stella laughed. Never in her wildest dreams had she imagined anything like this.

"Yes," George said, "it's a big deal to have this crossing of the river here by the bridge. Everyone talked about it for hundreds of kilometers around when the construction works started."

Stella hardly paid attention to his last words and stared at the structure ahead on top of the hill. What a magnificent castle."

"Surely no enemy can approach such high walls and towers reaching to the sky." Philip sat up straighter in the saddle. "I feel so small in comparison."

"In fact, the enemy would just turn around and leave if anyone ever tried to storm us." George smiled and winked. "It would be totally pointless to attempt. This elevated location was chosen on purpose. The steep bank of the river Sil we just crossed provides natural defense and a great source of water for the settlement."

"How genius!" Philip took in the unbreachable system of massive incredibly tall walls extending from an even taller square tower on the corner. The castle builder perfectly positioned two round turrets with narrow openings for the defending archers and their bows on either side of the main gate. "I always enjoyed visiting old castles, but never expected to see an operational one." The outside defensive wall construction displayed tooth-like construction with wider openings. Probably for throwing rocks and stones on the attackers. To be followed by boiling oil. "This time warp situation is proving to be very interesting, but we are in some gruesome century!"

"Because the Templar order is both monks and knights, our domain has features of both a castle and a monastery. It is superbly defensible and strategically placed. Inside, we have a church, a cloister and a dormitory." George signaled to the guards at the top of the approach ramp as they crossed a short drawbridge. The guards looked solemn and unshakable in their black tunics. As the riders moved inside, Philip noticed every detail of the giant pulley system for the drawbridge and the thickness of the main entry gate. The horses turned right up the inner ramp between the outside wall and the higher internal wall Philip noticed earlier.

Stella giggled and waved to the puzzled guards who didn't question their commander. Don't think you are the only confused people here. How long are we gonna be here in this time warp? "Señor George, can you tell me about the black and white colors of your shields. I see the same on the flag over there."

"Black is on top because evil and dark forces sometimes tip the scale in their favor. White is underneath to demonstrate that the good is ever-present and, overtime, the light will shine on all faces of humanity." He emphasized the words *good* and *light* by raising his right hand.

"That's kinda scary, though bright and beautiful at the same time…" Stella saw a man in a tunic with a wooden bucket of water in one hand. Many more inhabitants tended to their chores up ahead.

"We leave you here for now." George dismounted and helped everyone down near one of the stone huts with roofs of tightly thatched straw.

"Welcome! Come in!" A man from the castle's support staff invited them in without hesitation. "Our simple meal of freshly baked bread and warm garlic soup is waiting for you. It's just a little spicy. Feel free to relax over here if you like." Sleeping quarters were discernable in a room on a side.

"This will work!" Stella lay down on a mattress smelling of sweet grass. Sleeping in a real castle! Just look around this place." She jumped up and twirled in the main room of the hut.

"This bread is delicious!" Artur stuffed a piece in his mouth and scooped up the warm soup with another.

"Don't forget that George invited to show us around after the meal. Let's go ask for him and explore this self-contained city!" Philip savored the last bit of his soup and licked the spoon clean.

Life inside the castle walls was just like a humming old town. George led them through the bustle of peasant-looking folks carrying baskets of bread, sacks of potatoes and dividing some type of grain into smaller sacks. Chickens clucked in their wire cages and a woman in a kerchief covering her head was milking a goat nearby.

Alejandro squeezed his way closer and nearly shouted to Stella. "The goats are way smaller than ours on..." A man pulling a cart full of heavy vessels bumped into Alejandro who flailed his arms and knocked over the man's hat. The hat flew off his head and landed in the dust. Like a wild hunting animal, Tiger leaped on it and attacked the decorative feather. The man squeezed the handles of his cart. Everyone watched the demise of the feather in slow motion.

Philip wrestled the mostly undamaged hat – it was missing most of the feather – from Tiger and tentatively handed it to the man. "So sorry about the hat! Is that milk? Can we have some for our cat?" The man held his hat tight under his arm as he scooped up some milk and cautiously placed the cup on the ground. He scrutinized the unexpected attacker as Tiger finished his treat and wiped his face clean with a paw. Rubbing against the man's leg mended the whole situation.

"Thanks so much for the milk!" Stella scooped up Tiger.

"You are very welcome! Enjoy your afternoon." The man continued with his mission with firm steps and a determined look.

George led the group to the military preparation area located some distance from the chaos they just escaped. "Our order of warrior monks was formed in Jerusalem to protect the pilgrims making the voyage to the Holy Land. The Knights then had very few resources and our emblem showed two knights riding on a single horse due to poverty. Eventually, the order grew in membership and influence as many members of the noble families wanted to join our cause. The Knights were even granted the ability to pass freely across all borders."

"I heard about very strict rules of conduct members of your order have to follow." Philip caught up to George.

"You could say so. Among the rules is that Knights can eat only three times per week and have to take all our meals in silence."

"That would make you tough as steel!" Philip focused on George's muscular hands.

"Look at that sword! That's very cool!" Artur stepped closer to a man sharpening and polishing a very long shiny sword.

"Bet you couldn't lift it even with both arms." Stella never missed an opportunity for a friendly jab at her brother, but Artur was too entranced in the process.

"It's very important for us to be ready for battle at any moment. Each Knight can have three or four horses and hired squires to help with all the needs in the cavalry and heavy armor, but squires are not members of the order." George went over to examine a helmet his squire polished.

"Can I try it on?" Artur's eyes beamed with excitement.

"Here you go! See how that fits." George placed the heavy hunk of steel on Artur's head.

"This thing is awesome, but so uncomfortable. Where are you guys?" Artur turned his whole body looking through the eye slats in the helmet.

"You sound like a tin man from Wizard of Oz." Alejandro held his belly and pointed at Artur.

"I am King Artur!" He stepped forward and drew an imaginary sword.

George patted little knight on the back. "You look very authentic, especially considering that the legends of King Artur mention his sword, Excalibur, having an image of a cross with equal sides, similar to our Templar cross."

A group of men in black cloaks with a red cross approached as they led a pack of horses. "Sir, all horses' shoes have been checked for strength and fit. We are taking them to the stables now for rest and grooming."

"Well done, sergeants." George dismissed them with a motion of his hand. "Sergeants fight alongside the Knights as light cavalry. Very importantly, they have essential trade skills such as blacksmithing, building and carpentry to support the Knights in our daily lives."

"I wish Tiago were here!" Stella watched the horses and admired their sturdy gait.

"Surely he will turn up soon. Cheer up! Usually, only the guards can go up and around the castle walls, but you all are special, so follow me." George led the way up the narrow stone steps to the wall surrounding the castle and its many structures.

"No wonder this location has been chosen! What a view of the whole valley and the surrounding hills!" Philip took in the view and made a mental note of the hills they would cross soon on their trek.

"We could see anyone approaching to create a commotion in the area. The province of Galicia is out that way." He pointed over the mountains. "You will have to pass the high point in O Cebreiro. Expect colder wind and rain up there. We will give you some warm gear before you set out. Right now, you all look like you are out for an afternoon stroll instead of heading over the mountains to Santiago. Let's go up higher for a better look." George bent down to enter the narrow opening and everyone snaked after him. "Watch out, this stone staircase is very tight."

"Only one person could go up through the narrow steps. If anyone is coming down, we'd wait at the bottom to let them out. This platform at the top is quite spacious." Alejandro was the last one up. The watchman at the top greeted them – news of their arrival got around the castle.

"That curious shadow of the tower on the ground below looks like the towers in chess sets. Our shadows are on the ground too, and they are waving back!" Artur frantically flailed his arms and laughed.

"See the black roofs of the houses outside. This slate is mined locally. As you head out west into Galicia, you would almost not recognize the color because of the moss growing on the tiles. Tiles look nearly all green there yet black and shiny here in Leon province. In Galicia, the vegetation is bright green because of the rain they get on the other side of the mountains. So be ready, you may get wet!" George let them walk ahead of him along the fortified wall.

They walked around the perimeter of the castle, way above the daily hustle, and saw a wooden contraption at the wall opening. "I know! This is a catapult!" Artur grinned from ear to ear and ran his hand along the central wooden beam. "It looks complicated to operate but propels stones at the enemy outside the walls. Wow, look at the thickness of these ropes, Philip." Philip nodded and examined it more closely. Not that it surprised Stella, her brother wanted to be an engineer. He always analyzed how things worked.

"Never know when you may need it. We keep the rock pile fully stocked," George joked. Now I'll show you a special place in the castle that only select few have access to. You have demonstrated much composure so far and judgement beyond your years."

George led them down another set of steep steps. On the ground, Alejandro followed the commander so closely, he nearly stepped on George's foot. Soon they came into a large room with only a few windows and huge wooden shelves, full of books, floor to ceiling.

"So many books!" Stella spun around, looking from one wall to another. "What an extra special place! Think of all the ancient knowledge, all the information, all the pictures, all the ... everything!" Stella didn't know where to look first.

"Yes, that's why we call this place *templum libri*, the temple of books. If you want to look at something you can't reach, just ask this attendant. I must get back to some important duties now. You all can stay here as long as you want. Can you find your way back?"

"Yes." Stella nodded still trying to take it all in.

"See you later then!" George left them to explore the world of ancient knowledge and mysteries.

Gift of Treasure

10

"You can spend days here, weeks, even years, there are so many books. There are some on the table here. Let's see what they are!" Stella lifted a heavy wooden chair closer to the expansive table in the middle of the room. She placed it softly and climbed up close to three open books. All of them were leather-bound and very old-looking. So old, you would think they should be in a museum under glass. But it's clearly ok to look through them.

Stella leaned over a thick book with *Herbolarium* spelled out in large letters on the cover. Each fragile page showed signs of age and brownish areas along the edges. Detailed drawings of various botanicals captivated Stella. She poured over plant parts – roots, stems, leaves, flowers, fruits and attempted to read various cures and potions associated with each plant. *It must be in Latin…Some words are so familiar, and some are puzzling, the script is so consistent. How did they handwrite the whole book without any variations?* What a beautiful world of plants, some familiar, some completely unknown to her.

"The colors and the details are stunning! Wow!" Stella carefully flipped the pages. "This entire world of treasure in the herbal medicine all around us. We just don't notice it. We just walk right past the common chamomile, mint, calendula and lavender. We think of them just as pretty or fragrant plants, but they hold so much healing power." She finally lifted her head and turned to Philip with the eyes still glazed over.

"Would love to hear more later." Philip immersed himself in the astronomy book right next to Stella. "Look here - stars, planets, constellations alive on each page. Summer and winter solstice, spring and fall equinoxes, calculations for the lunar cycles, trajectories of Venus and Mars… Here is an astrolabe, an ancient tool used for navigation. It considered the altitude of celestial bodies above the horizon." He pointed to a circular drawing with many inscriptions and notches around the circumference. "Nowadays, it seems common knowledge, yet ancient astronomers performed all these calculations and observations by hand over countless sleepless nights observing the celestial bodies and their eternal dance in our skies. They recorded and classified this ancient movement that carries so much grace and poise in its unstoppable dance. I can feel the determination of astronomers of old who passed on the works of their lives for everyone to appreciate and use." He sighed.

"All these pages and pages with calculations, drawings, schematics… The plant language is easier for me to understand." Stella flipped to another page in her book. It pictured various parts of the rose plant and described the healing qualities of rose hips.

"Yeah, the language of math and scientific observation is not for everyone. Oh, I've never thought of it this way…" Philip pulled the heavy book closer and his chair squeaked.

"Look here, this is interesting. See these dots that make a bow or figure 8 placed sideways."

"The sign for infinity?" Stella leaned over.

"Exactly! This drawing depicts the position of the sun in the sky at various times in the year. We are so dependent on the cycles of the sun. The sun is our manifestation of eternity and infinite life cycles on this planet." Philip leaned back and hooked his arm over the back of the chair. "It shines the light against the darkness of velvet depth of space to support life on this planet."

"I'm gonna need to remember to say good morning to the sun and give thanks to it each day." Stella placed her hand on her heart and took a deep breath.

"What did you guys find?" Philip turned to Artur and Alejandro huddled over a book with gold-leaf pages and ornate paintings.

"*The Bestiario*, the book with ancient mythical animals, full of legends and myths. Check out the dragons and unicorns! And this one animal whose name I don't know." Alejandro pointed to a page with a mythical beast of charcoal gray color with a body like a lion's, big claws and spikes. Its spur-like shielding ran up each leg all the way to the knee joint.

"Hmmm, I don't know either." Philip leaned over for a better look.

"It has some kind of scales, triangular looking protection pieces on its chest. The scales continue from the chest up the neck in a way of a mane and all the way over his head." Artur traced the outline of the beast with his finger. "The tail is whipped up over his back and also has scaly spikes on it."

"Look at that face, such a big grin with large white teeth and almost human eyes. He is a mischievous troublemaker." The animal caught Stella's attention.

"He is on the next page too, sitting on his hind legs." Alejandro flipped the page gently. "This time on a shield of a nobleman or a king wearing a crown and riding a horse in some fancy regalia. This dragon-lion must have been very smart and powerful if ancient royalty depicted him on the shields."

"Maybe was a very powerful protector but could change his mind at any moment if angered or displeased." Stella ran her over the gold-leaf flower. "How do you make friends with a beast so moody and work with him by your side?"

It grew dark and the library attendant lit candles for them, but he eventually gently waved them on and pulled the door shut. Everyone walked out of *templum libri* without saying much. They made their way through the grounds of the quieting castle community. Torches were burning and only a few inhabitants moved slowly about their business.

"That library is a place of treasures and mysteries we can't even fathom. Wish we could spend more time here." All the plants and potions and remedies just in one book. How much more is out there?! Stella sighed and kept pace with her big brother's sizable steps.

"If I could read Greek, Latin or Arabic, I could learn so much more," Philip said.

"All those magical creatures we found in the book... I am getting tired." Artur cuddled on the straw mattress in the hut with Tiger at his feet. Alejandro prepared his bed near him.

"It's warm, let's sit outside and enjoy the night." Stella wasn't ready for bed quite yet. "What else did you learn about, Philip?"

"Funny you should ask about it exactly now. I read the astronomy book and look at these stars! Just can't get enough of them." Philip leaned back to enjoy the sky. "It's hard to see them so clearly while living in the city. The city lights obscure them and only the brightest are visible." He sighed. "Sometimes I feel kinda disconnected from others in the big city, even with so many people around me. Everyone is rushing about their business, not paying much attention to what is going on around them. Here, in the middle of nowhere, with people from a different century we barely met, I feel more at ease and quite comfortable with the darkness. The starlight is actually very calming."

"I think so too..." Alejandro yawned.

"Here you can see some of the constellations I read about. Look at Polaris, they call it the pole star, the north star or the guiding star. You can find Polaris if you follow the handle stars of the Little Dipper, Ursa Minor." Philip pointed with his hand. "What we see as one-star Polaris from here is actually a combination of two stars orbiting the third star." Philip drew a dot in the dust with a circle around it and placed two dots near each other on the circle. "Polaris is visible in the northern hemisphere and doesn't change its location. The rest of the celestial sphere seems to rotate around it. That's how the navigators of ships and caravans could always tell which way they went. I read today that over many centuries the earth's celestial pole, where Polaris is now, changed its location. The pole used to point to a slightly different area nearby because of various influences on the tilt in the earth's rotation." He lifted his index finger and moved it in a circle. "Some ancient astronomers described the celestial pole as devoid of any stars at all."

"Polaris was just regular star back then probably." Stella hung on to every word Philip said. He knows so much about the celestial bodies.

"There is a shooting star falling from Orion's belt!" Alejandro jumped up and pointed. "Did you see that? Make a wish, make a wish."

"I wish… I wish many more people could experience the treasured moments like this, outside, looking at the stars. I wish they could feel more connected to their families, other people and the whole big world. I wish they could find comfort in looking at the big sparkly sky. I wish they could always hear the stars, the sun, and the moon telling them: *"Everything will be ok, we have been here for a long time. We know it's true. Believe in the magic inside of you and find the way to connect with the big magic outside."*

"That's a beautiful wish, Philip." Stella hugged her brother. "Hope it comes true. The stars will make sure of it."

"Now let's get inside and see some magical dreams. Good night, my pilgrim crew." Philip ushered Alejandro and Stella inside.

BEAUTY WITHIN 11

"Good morning pilgrims!" George stood at the door of their hut. "Would you like some help looking for your horse?"

"We sure would, since you know the area well." Alejandro jumped to his feet.

"I can show you around too, there are some nice fields south of here. Maybe he wandered that way. There is a secret shortcut we can take." George winked and led everyone down to the cellar with a small door camouflaged behind some large barrels. "Grab a torch everyone."

"Smells musty!" Stella scrunched up her nose as they headed down into an underground passage. "Where is this leading?"

"This is our escape route, just in case of extreme emergency and if we cannot defend the castle. Don't tell anyone, but this puts us a safe distance away in Castrillo de Cornatel." George burned a few cobwebs as he walked. "Here we are, watch your heads." George propped the door open and everyone popped out into another cellar with stone walls and ceiling. George nodded to the guards outside. "Let's go up to the tower and look for Tiago."

They stood at the top of the hill looking down, just like they did in the castle in Ponferrada. Squinting against the sun, Stella carefully examined the valley. "Nothing! Let's go walk around, maybe he will turn up." They walked around most of the day amid tall grass fields with bright red-orange poppies in bloom. The birds chirped in the branches of oak and birch trees. Eucalyptus and pine popped up here and there, but not as abundantly as they had seen in other areas.

George led them with the familiarity of a local very comfortable in his surroundings. Coming out of the thicket on a bank of a river, he uncovered a small rowboat, carefully camouflaged under a bush. "Let's take this along the river for a while. Maybe he is somewhere near looking for water." George kept the boat steady as they stepped in and Tiger squirmed in Philip's shoulder bag.

Everyone piled in and took up small wooden paddles which they used mainly for steering the boat. The current of the river did most of the work carrying the tiny vessel downstream. The clouds gathered slowly over the course of the day and their friend, the wind, came along eventually. Small waves jumped over the surface, rocking the boat gently on its way. Over time, the wind got stronger and the swells got bigger. The wind swished at them sideways, threatening to topple over the boat and tumble them into the river.

"Look, there's an eddy of calm water near the bank where the river bulges on the side a little. Let's turn over there, past those cattails and under that willow tree." George steered the boat with his paddle and motioned everyone to paddle on one side.

The soft, gentle and bendy branches of the willow embraced the little boat in its canopy. They suddenly found themselves in a very calm protected space. The water bugs skimmed along the surface of the water, fish came up from time to time and tried to catch the bugs. The frogs made their throaty noises on the shore and the crickets chimed in but kept their distance from the frogs.

"The cattails and the willow make a perfect resting spot, don't they?" Artur rested his paddle on his lap and wiped his forehead.

"Yes, who would have thought? How did you know to look for it here, George?" Philip squeezed his paddle between his knees and leaned his chin on it.

"Well, it's part of training your eyes and your other senses. When you know these places exist, you will always be able to find them. Whenever a storm rages outside or in your life, you just try to picture this place of calm and peace waiting for you. You can always "pull over" and wait out the storm in safety. Here you can ask for clarity and guidance on where to go next. You don't have to battle the currents or the wind in this protected area. You can focus on asking the questions about what is of the most importance. What steps can you take to come out safely from the storm? What direction to take next?" George looked at each of them.

"It is not only a physical location, but a quiet space inside of you." Alejandro's eyes lit up.

"You can get here easily once you know the feeling of belonging in it." George smiled. "It's always available, no matter what troubles rage outside. It's your personal beautiful space within yourself where everything is in balance and harmony.

It's the place where the waters are calm. It's a place of certainty that the current of the river and the flow of life will take you exactly where you need to go."

"As long as you pay attention and steer your boat in the direction of your calling…" Philip ran his hand along the bendy willow branches above his head.

George watched the water bug skim along the water surface. "You can listen to the messages that appear to you and watch the signs that come up in this quiet space. When you are ready, you steer out into the open and go where you need to go. Know that you will be safe and can always pull over again for a little rest if you need to."

"It should be safe to go now, the wind really calmed down." Stella lifted the paddle from her lap.

"There is an outpost here along this bend. We can ask them for a ride back to the castle since it's getting late. We can try looking for Tiago again tomorrow. For today, let's make sure to be safe and not get into harm by searching in the dark." George pushed the willow branches out of the way and gave the boat a powerful start with his paddle.

"Well, we know how ineffective looking in the dark can be!" Artur laughed, remembering their search and spending the night outside in the forest.

"Row, row, row your boat, gently down the stream," Stella hummed with each paddle stroke.

"Merrily, merrily, merrily, life is but a dream." Alejandro whistled and checked for his flute in his pocket. "Haven't played for you guys recently."

Together at Last

12

It had been a few days without Tiago. Stella refused to give up, not that Philip or Artur wanted to, no, they all wanted to find him. The time switch still amazed all of them. Yet, they had somewhat ceased being surprised by it.

"Who knows, maybe Tiago took off to meet his old equine friends with whom he rode in the battles of the 11th century. Or maybe they weren't horses then but unicorns with colorful sparkling manes and flowing graceful tails." Stella ran her hand through her hair and flipped it up.

"Your imagination works overtime." Alejandro chuckled.

"Maybe his best friend was a Pegasus boasting the awesome power of his strong wings capable of carrying him to the viewpoint from just below the clouds. That would be an enormous advantage to anyone of course – to exist on the earth plane and to be capable of soaring above the daily battles to gain a higher perspective on things." Artur put his palm to shield his eyes from the sun. "In any case, Tiago probably chose some notable characters for his company. I love riding that powerful horse, it makes me feel like a mighty Knight and a noble warrior."

"Nobility and magnificent strength don't come from training and endurance alone. Winning insights come from the power of observation and connection with the magical things all around." Alejandro fingered the holes of his flute. "Often I just pay attention to the position of the birds on electric wires leading to the village. They look like musical notes perched in dark silhouettes against the blue sky. Sometimes, I write the notes down and play the music of nature on my flute."

"Your music is lovely. So many people compliment you on the charming melodies cheering everyone up. Now we know your secret." Stella smiled and patted her friend on the back. "How you care for your sheep reflects your attentive ways too. You don't rush them against their will but gently guide them to the best pastures with the tasty grass. In the evenings, it seems you are in charge of them, leading them home."

"Truthfully, I just follow them. They trust me to let them out of their paddocks the next morning in their search for tasty grass. Watching them, I learned to relax the death grip I applied to my flute when I just started playing." Alejandro balanced a small rock on top of another. "I miss my wooly friends…"

"Maybe this inner trust and your connection to the ways of nature can help us to reunite with Tiago eventually." Stella held her breath and blew it out slowly.

"We know Tiago is a horse, a very smart horse. Even though we got separated from him in a wooden thicket, Tiago is used to living with people and walking on roads." Alejandro balanced another rock on the cairn. "When Stella takes him for a ride, she doesn't go bushwhacking in the forest. Tiago is friendly and always allows pilgrims to pet him on his handsome face and those muscular front legs."

Stella nodded. "He usually stops and neighs when he sees other farmers with their horses on the Way."

"So…" Philip leaned in and swallowed.

"I know where to look for Tiago!" Alejandro surprised everyone. "I was just watching the ants determinately carry their loads. They go in the same direction – to their home. Tiago will know where his brothers are. All we must do is get him in this timeframe. After that, I know where to look."

"Seems plausible. How do you suppose we can do that?" Philip shifted back and forth.

"Make our own magic!" Stella smirked. She could definitely try this new game. "We can will him to appear in this timeline. Haven't thought of this before, but until now we believed that we were all lost, which is not true. We came in our wanderings exactly to the place where Knights rested near the pond. We know it was for a reason. We can find the power we didn't know we had. The Camino has magic, I heard those stories from many pilgrims in our courtyard at home. When we use this magic with our intentions, we can bring Tiago closer to us."

"One, two, three…" Artur threw the flat stone on the cobblestones, to make it skip like on the flat surface of the lake.

"That's it! I know! Artur, please give me that stone and I'll show you a trick." Philip stretched his open palms for a catch.

"Ok… Here you go!" Artur tossed Philip a stone.

Philip studied the smooth stone for a few seconds, flipping it and rolling it in his hands. He rubbed it and blew on it a little to shake off the dust. "Oh, I get it now. It's our breath, it carries our intentions. Do you want to find our horse, Artur? Here, wish very strongly that he comes to us soon. Imagine petting him, giving him an apple. You know he will beg for carrots after the apple."

"I can do that; I would love to feed him!" Artur squeezed his eyelids tight, made smacking noises with his lips like he was calling Tiago, blew on the stone and then offered it to the others.

Stella and Alejandro, in turn, closed their eyes and appeared to be petting Tiago on his face. They both blew on the stone one after another. Philip smiled, closed his eyes and blew on the stone. "Then how to connect our intentions with the Camino magic?" He bent his knees and did exactly what Artur had done a few minutes ago. He skipped the shiny wishing stone on the cobblestones. It bounced three times and disappeared on the side of the path. A few bugs scampered from the grass. A butterfly nobody noticed flew up from that area, fluttered its beautiful iridescent wings and went on about its flying business.

"Nicely done! Now follow me." Alejandro had a mysterious smile on his face.

"To where?" Stella got to her feet.

"Just trust me. Trust is important, we don't always have all the answers. Just believe..." Alejandro winked.

"Who are these kids, really? How do they know this stuff?" Philip stared at the two friends walking hand in hand down the path as the Camino joined a bigger gravel road that led them back to the town of Ponferrada. Alejandro headed straight for the castle and then the stables. Solemn guards stepped aside as he marched confidently past them.

"Are you joking?" Philip laughed.

The attendant at the stables nearly ran out to them waving his hands. "Not too long ago a new horse wandered in." He caught his breath. "He went straight for the last spot where George's horse is, just like old buddies or something. I bet he is your Tiago!" He handed them apples and oranges.

"Tiago! Tiago!" Stella screamed and ran towards a familiar neigh. The boys followed close behind. "We did it! We did it!" She jumped and twirled in her pink butterfly dress.

"Good boy, Tiago! Good boy!" Artur petted him and fed him apples.

"How can this be possible?" Philip ran his fingers through Tiago's thick mane.

"Told you, it's magic!" Stella smacked his arm and laughed. She hugged her horse around the neck. "You're back! Together again on the Camino!"

Dragons in Armor

13

"Our crew is complete again!" Artur ran first to tell George the good news.

"Didn't doubt it for a second that you would find your noble steed. You have special powers!" George watched the excited youngsters gather all around.

"Thanks for helping us look for him! It's great to have him with us. I am so happy; I could give you a hug. But I know it's against the Knights rules." Stella smiled radiantly at George and he bowed his head in gratitude.

"We found Tiago, but it feels like something remains to be done before we can continue on our way..." Alejandro tapped on the flute sticking out from his pants pocket. He gazed at the distant gentle cloud in the sky for a few moments. "I can't quite put my finger on it. Maybe I'll take some time to play and think it over." He sat down on the ground in the middle of the castle courtyard.

"We can hang around and enjoy your music. Haven't heard you play for some time." Philip made himself comfortable on the ground and motioned to Stella and Artur to join him. George stood a little back, resting one hand on his hip and watching Alejandro intently. Alejandro drifted off, unaware of all the attention on him as he closed his eyes and drew in a deep breath. The first crisp notes floated effortlessly from the little flute as the melodic heartsong rose from somewhere deep inside. He gave his full attention to the inhaling breath expanding his lungs, vibrating all through his body, filling his belly. When his breath flowed into the flute, as if by magic, the stream of air turned into beautiful soulful sounds.

Alejandro let the music pour out from him, inspired by the adventures, the nature and the fun he had with his friends along the way. The song was his own creation, which came to him in this moment, stirred up by the highs and the lows of the hills and valleys around him. His fingers hovered above the flute's finger holes and danced up and down for each note as he stepped and leaped over the musical scale with ease and grace. He pulsed his finger quickly over the bottom hole creating a trill. A series of chirps and turns followed in combinations that reached out to everyone nearby and floated far into the clouds.

Stella nudged Artur to point out a few Knights and sergeants who stood nearby. They too halted their conversation and observed Alejandro. He changed the pitch in barely noticeable ways over the course of his musical prayer as he varied the intensity of his breath. He sometimes slid and rolled the fingers over the openings to create an almost longing effect.

"It's like he is reaching out all the way up and calling someone to come down," Stella whispered to Philip.

"Sounds so deep, profound and intense." Philip admired the young musician's inspired skill.

"What are the Knights doing? Look how they have their palms turned out and their eyes closed." Stella gazed in the direction of the group.

"They are holding space for Alejandro to do his work, supporting him by sending positive vibes. They are sensing something important. Even George has his eyes closed too, looks like he is praying..." Philip started humming deeply in his throat.

Meanwhile, Alejandro pulsed his breath and created a lower pitch and volume, allowing the flute to vibrate deeply. He breathed in slowly and steadily, slowing down even more at the end of each musical phrase.

"That really pulls on the heartstrings," George murmured as a series of bluesy notes floated up and all the air flowed through one open hole at the top of the flute.

Stella hummed under her breath "Aa, aaa, aaa a a ...."

While Artur examined the details of the Knights' outfits, something unusual caught his eye in the sky. He raised his finger to point but put his hand down as his jaw dropped open. "Over there."

Alejandro lost track of time as he followed the soaring energy of his tune. He continued to play when he opened his eyes from a dream-like state, looking out but not really focusing on anything. But he found it hard to ignore the scene unfolding in front of him. *Am I really seeing this?* He really wished he could rub his eyes, but his hands were occupied, so he kept on playing. His eyes opened wider and wider and he drew in another breath, repeating the last musical verse. It's like the melody reaches from the sky deep into the earth's core and connects with the pull of the earth, he thought. Alejandro played on and on, leery to spook the mirage that attracted everyone's attention by then.

Dragons swarmed the castle! These immense creatures dropped from the sky! Some appeared bigger than the surrounding hills, some smaller, like a second rank, Alejandro noted. He held the last note longer and slowly unsealed his lips from the mouthpiece. He rested the enigmatic flute on his lap and looked around with eyes wide open. Each dragon rested on a turret or a tower. And they didn't land with a thud, no – they landed quietly, their barely visible shapes existed on the edge of reality. They created a distortion in the air as they approached and paused their movement above their goal and destination.

"The dragons are one of a kind army and their armor is stronger than ever known on this planet. Creators and protectors of dreams. They swoop in whenever someone imagines and takes steps to realize their dreams." George stepped closer to the children. "Dreams are the sacred goals brought down to this reality from beyond. Beyond the sky, beyond the starlight. The dreams are the inspired messages we remember from that far beyond, seemingly unattainable at first."

"Really?" Stella glanced over her shoulder at the closest dragon and put one hand on her belly and one on her chest.

"Dreams are the moment in space when we remember our divine connections to that faraway beyond. It's the inspiration that comes on the wings of a dragonfly. They are connected – the dragonflies and the dragons."

"No way! That dragonfly we saw by the pond…" Alejandro stood up slowly.

"Though different in their perceived size, they carry equally important responsibilities. People can receive inspiration in anything they want by perceiving a dragonfly in the palm of their receiving hand, usually the left hand. Dragonflies will appear in an instance or an eternity, as those are also relative. In a warm feeling of energy flowing in a palm of your hand, dragonflies will be the messenger of things to come." Stella rubbed the palm of her left hand as George continued. "Your dreams are the things you will bring to light of this world. Trust them, as they are divinely inspired, carried to the person across the vast expanse of the universe to bring lightness and likeness to your heart, to remind where you come from. To know you are safe where you are going."

"Do dreams really come true?" Artur stepped up closer to George.

"It will be how you imagined it among the stars. They will come alive with your will and dedication to your divine purpose of the visit on the earth… this time in the karmic cycle and the dance of the moons."

"Do you mean moons or moon?" Philip perked up.

"Moons of the earth are multiple; their movement sets the flows and balances of energies destined for creative thinking. Only one moon is illuminated for all to see. Others are to be known and perceived with your heart and inner mind. The dance of the moons can be adjusted like the giant clock with levers in a certain position." George raised one arm and pulled it down pushing the other arm up.

"We as humans collectively pull those levers to transition through our destiny." George walked about and stopped in front of Philip. "The solar wind charges these moons with love for all living beings. Depending on the distribution of the charge, the balance and position of the moons changes and can even tip the magnetic poles! For a blank page restarting the cycle of education for all…"

"That's gonna take me some time to digest." Philip rubbed his temple.

"The solar wind is not a barrage of bursts. It's a gentle purposeful flow of energy ions set in motion over ions of time. This notion connects energy, matter and time simply by using this concept of their relativity to each other. Ions as tiny particles of matter are brothers of tiny particles of time, related to each other and all of us by their origin in the heart of space time." George looked down and smiled at Stella.

"Hey there, tiny brother in time!" Stella grinned at Artur.

"Only an inch more to grow and I will be calling you little sister soon, my dear sister in time." Artur put both hands on his hips, straightened his back, raised his chin and smirked.

George held back a smile. "Space is our ability and destiny to create. Time is providing the incentive to keep moving through that creative process. We are the children of the Creator's dream set in motion by curiosity. That dream is us created. That dream is us creating." He focused on everyone in turn, letting the words sink in. "Next, we gain consciousness of this process and the ability to rely on our strength, to ask for support from the moons and bring more dragonflies into our hand. When we do that, love comes eternally without order or the numbering of the pages of our lives."

"Sounds like the dragonfly is a symbol of the power of each specific thought, divinely inspired with love and beauty. The dragons are in their armor to protect this process within each conscious heart." Stella had a gleam in her eyes and a knowing grin.

"Wow, the Camino has really offered us many gifts of time and thoughtfulness." Philip put a hand around his sister's shoulder as she leaned in and hugged him around his waist.

A sergeant approached the group. "I sensed earlier that as the dragons swarmed in today to the towers of the secure castle, they had a specific vision to protect."

"What did you note? I missed a lot whole in my own world, playing." Alejandro shifted his weight from one foot to another.

"The dream that you and the Knights are creating together for a peaceful world. The world where all are protected and nobody is afraid of their thoughts censored or corrected, of their freedom to create taken away." The sergeant stepped back a little.

George took over the idea. "The world of how you see things with your young minds, with the rainbow colors getting brighter and the flowers spreading on the hill in their spontaneous bloom."

"We can share this vision together in the safety of each other, in the courage of the Knights from another era, in the beauty and love surrounding this moment of eternity where everything is one. That's my dream." Stella admired the dragons on the castle wall.

"There are so many of them, on the turrets, on the walls, waiting intently, pausing their breath for this gentle moment of a dream come true." Alejandro stretched his arms out. "Look, some are even on the ground within the walls, coming closer to our mismatched group of dreamers."

"Because of this special circumstance, it is possible to observe the dragons and dragonflies in their beautiful work and not feel afraid." George gently bowed his head to the dragon closest to them in a gesture of gratitude and recognition. The dragon accepted that gift and passed it on to his companions. It translated into the gentle tap-tap of the spiky tails on the stones of the castle walls.

"The sound is so surreal given that the dragons are barely visible as a distortion of their shapes in the summer air." Alejandro shook his head.

"Who can't tell anymore the difference between strange, magic, and the dream of this purple dragonfly." Stella stretched out her hand. She glanced at the dragonfly and smiled. "My favorite color is pink, but it would be too much to present a pink dream to this group of medieval Knights, my brothers, my friend, and the cat."

"Oh, let's not forget the cat in all of this. Looking like the master of ceremonies, sitting on his back legs and majestically distributing his weighty fluff around the cobblestone, warming in the sun." Philip scratched Tiger behind his ears. "Did you know this would happen? Did you orchestrate it? Oh Tiger, you have been in our family for such a long time." Tiger only squinted and purred in response.

Tiago grazed on the grass nearby, cautiously observing all the dragons. Artur went over and held tight to his reins. "Want to make sure you are safe this time and don't fall into a wormhole again. Hope I don't get dragged in..."

"Time will tell, space will show how this all works out," George said softly.

"As of now, we are together looking at this pink, sorry, purple dragonfly." Philip took a few steps and glanced from the dragonfly to the nearest dragon.

"Well, make a wish, make it good." Stella raised her open palm. "*Uno, dos, tres,* fly for the beauty in the world," she instructed the dragonfly.

"Fly for the peace of all living beings." Philip put a hand on his heart.

"Fly for the joy and happiness of the eternal magic of creation," Alejandro said.

"Mmmm, fly for the sweetness in the air and the warmth of the loving sun." George held his hands together in prayer.

"Fly for the fun of all kids and adults playing joyfully together." Artur clapped his hands.

"Ready, dragonfly?" Stella held out her hand.

The dragonfly acquired more color in its wings. "Everyone, take a deep breath and exhale gently and purposefully towards the dragonfly. In this manner, we let our intentions be known to it and the world." George put a hand on his heart, and they followed his motion. Dragonfly's wings moved fast and decisively as it took off to the open sky. Stella blew him a kiss. The dragons moved their wings forward, gently supporting it on its way up, encouraging it with all their dedication to their duty. Soon the dragonfly vanished way up high. The dragons bowed in gratitude for the blessing they supported. Their job as the protectors of the special creative moment was complete and they took off, soon disappearing in a cloud over the hills.

Philip broke the silence. "Ok then, who's hungry?" Philip rubbed his hand together and everyone laughed.

Been There Done That   14

"Look at all your smiles! I think you are ready to go! Did you pack the food?" George looked over the young pilgrims.

"Of course, we are ready! Tiago is back!" Artur held on to the reins.

"He is a beautiful strong horse; glad he is back with you. You all made some friends here even during such a short visit." George and other Knights cheered and patted Tiago for good luck. "Buen Camino! Wave to us from Santiago! If you have some extra time, stop by Las Medulas, the abandoned Roman gold mines. There is no more gold to be found, but the scenery is spectacular. Worth a stop while you are in the area." George requested the guards to lower the drawbridge.

"Thanks for your hospitality and protection! See you some time!" Philip gave a firm handshake to George.

"You said the word *time*... I think that's when things get funny with us." Alejandro barely smiled. "Hopefully, it will bring us back to our time."

"Buen Camino!" George waved and crossed the bridge behind them. He stopped on the threshold and watched the young pilgrims, their horse and cat move down the ramp, on their way out of the Templars' castle in Ponferrada and towards their mission in Santiago. "Blessed be!" He raised his right hand sending them good luck vibes as they headed west over the cobblestone road. He turned back to the gate towards the other Knights who all peered down the valley as the group disappeared out of sight. "Let's say a prayer for them inside." George rubbed his chest and cleared his throat. "Lift the bridge, close the gates." He spun around and emphasized each step on the way to the friary.

"Feels good to be on the road again! Watch out for those thorns, Stella. Still don't want your sneakers?" Big brother squeezed Stella's shoulders.

"It's fine, I will be careful." Stella kicked a small stone out of the way and marched on.

"We can take a lunch break at Las Medulas. Will be a good time to rest and check out the underground passages." Philip adjusted his backpack, now heavier with the generous provisions. "George said that at the top of the hill we will see the chestnut trees and lots of oaks. The mines are in the valley down below, where the dirt had been taken out. It's the only place in the area with the wind-blown towers of the red-orange soil."

"George said the Romans abandoned the mines centuries ago after a big flash flood washed out most of the operations and killed close to a thousand workers." Alejandro gestured to the hillside. "The water probably rushed from over there."

"They must have come close to depleting the land and took out most of the precious metals." Stella followed his gaze to the top of the hill.

"Do you hear that?" Philip stopped and blocked Stella's way with his hand. "What are all these grinding, metal crunching and chain rattling noises?"

"Sounds like the mines are fully operational. All the shouting is harsh!" Stella winced.

"Scoot over to the side!" Philip lowered his voice. "I hear a bunch of horses approaching too!" Philip grabbed Alejandro's clammy arm and gave Stella a small push behind the rocks. "Hurry guys! Artur, jump down from the horse." His voice cracked. He led Tiago behind a large rock outcropping and pressed his back against it. "Shhh!" Philip huddled with Artur, pressed his finger to his lips and peaked out. A bunch of heavy horse-drawn covered carts rolled down the road kicking up clouds of dust. The riders were dressed in short tunics with leather belt straps and leather sandals; swords dangled by their sides.

"Don't tell me…" Alejandro whispered. "Are we in a different timeframe again?"

"Though this time, let's try to avoid being seen. Don't have a good feeling about this." Stella hugged both arms around her body.

"Let's still check out the views as George recommended and get out of here before we're drafted to work in the mines ourselves." Philip took a better look up the road where the carts came from.

"No arguments from me!" Artur stayed behind a bush.

"Let's head over to the top of the hill along the scrub brush there. Tiago, are you going to be ok if we leave you to eat here?" Philip secured the reins as the horse already had his mouth full of grass. "Tiger, stay here to keep him company please." Tiger stretched out on a warm rock and turned his fluffy belly to the sun, exposing his white chin and the white fur on his chest.

"We can creep up in the shade of the chestnut trees, through those silvery-green bushes." Alejandro directed them uphill.

"I see a rock here on the ledge we can peek from. Careful everyone, stay down low." Philip unhooked the prickly bush branch that pulled on Stella's dress and looked her over for thorns.

They crouched as they watched a fully operational mining operation down below. Lots of pulleys and wagons carried piles of rock from under the ground. Tracks and shakers were set up for washing the soil and separating gold from rocks and dirt. Workers hustled and overseers shouted instructions, hurrying them to get the job done. Some tunnel openings darkened the side of the cliff and workers lowered buckets of soil with chains attached to a wooden contraption.

"All this commotion is in such jarring contrast to those calm earth formations." Stella pointed to the red rocks shaved down by rain and water to the skinny pillars. "Some are like large mounds with flat tops, some like giant teepees." Wherever the oak trees remained, their vivid green color contrasted the orangy-reds of the ground. "Impressive spot to visit. Farther out in the valley, there are no more reds, just fields and small hills." The view went far into the hills and eventually to the mountains they would cross on the journey to Santiago.

"Just a short way away, right?" Philip assessed the distance to the closest hill and located the path snaking through the valley.

"No worries, we'll skip some stones and get there in no time," Alejandro said.

"Now let's get out of here 'cause working in the mines under the supervision of Roman soldiers will delay our plans." Philip tapped Stella on the shoulder. "The view is awesome, but I don't want to attract attention since we are right on the canyon rim here." They scrambled down the hill, untied Tiago and with Tiger in hand made their way out of the area, talking in hushed voices.

"I wonder how we can control all these crazy time jumps we get into…" Stella turned to Philip.

"Not sure that we can. Seems like all we can do is be on our way to where we need to go. It's like things arrange themselves for us. Just gotta trust that we are always in the right place at the right time." Philip paused to listen to a bird chirping somewhere in the nearby bushes.

"Ouch! Darn it! Guys slow down!" Stella's face was pale, and she winced in pain.

"What's wrong?" Alejandro rushed over.

"It's bleeding!" Stella sat down, clutching her foot. "Must have been a sharp piece of slate sticking up somewhere."

"Let me see, we have to apply pressure on the wound to stop the bleeding." Philip knelt near her. "Give me that cloth the bread is wrapped in, it's the cleanest thing we have." He folded it over the spot on Stella's foot, where the blood pooled steadily, and held it tight for a few minutes. "Not wearing shoes has an upside of not getting blisters, but the downsides are obvious too. Does it hurt badly?"

"No, not that much... I don't... want to let you guys down." Stella sobbed. "What if I can't walk?" Tears rolled down her cheeks.

"If you can't walk, you can ride. But we can't fix this by worrying. Looks like the bleeding stopped, we can rinse it out with water now. Artur, there is a bottle in my pack, can you bring it please." Philip stroked Stella's hair and wiped her tears. "Here, all clean. Let's prop up your foot and let it air dry. "I'll rinse this out in a creek, we will need to bandage your foot when it dries."

"Are you feeling better?" Alejandro knelt and examined her wounded foot. "It's a long cut but doesn't seem deep. Will just have to keep it clean and hope for the best. If you can make it to the next village, we can get help. Don't worry. Want to eat something?" Alejandro pulled out the stash of food.

"Maybe later... Can you pass me Philip's jacket? This rock is a little hard." She felt the envelope in the inner pocket as she stuffed the jacket under her leg. "Why do you think your grandfather sealed the envelope he gave us?"

"Huh? Why do you worry about that now? We should think how to fix your foot so you can walk!" Alejandro sat up straighter.

"Well, exactly. Maybe there is something in the letter that will help us get to Santiago faster or easier…" She smoothed out her dress and rubbed her knee.

"It doesn't matter what's in the letter. We promised to deliver it intact. You wanted to go on the Camino so much, so why hurry now? You forget how much you talked about it every day at home?"

"Oh, I love being here! I was just curious…" She rolled a tiny stone in her hand. "I thought you would want to know too…"

"Well, then let's see what we can do about your foot and get to Santiago somehow. We will find out soon enough." Alejandro stretched his legs. "Remember, curiosity killed the cat."

"Guess you are right…" Stella leaned back on her elbows and kept her foot elevated on a rock. She turned her head to the side. "Wait a minute! Alejandro, can you grab that green plant leaf for me? The one with many fuzzy cuts."

"This thing over here?" He leaned over and snipped it from the stalk.

"It's the one!" Stella examined it closely. "I read about it at the Templar library! Achillea millefolium or yarrow."

"It looks like a thousand tiny dissected leaves." Alejandro turned the plant over and over in his hands.

"This plant is named after Achilles, the hero in Greek mythology. He used this plant to stop bleeding and heal the soldiers' wounds." Stella grinned. "The book said to crush the leaves and to squeeze out the juice around the wound. It barely even stings."

"How handy! Did they mention any other herbs to reduce swelling and infection?" Alejandro perked up.

"There were others, but I remember one very clearly, plantago major or plantain. They say it usually grows near a road or a path. I've seen them near our farm too but didn't know it was so special. It's been used since ancient times for various reasons, but its antiseptic and analgesic qualities are what we need."

"Huh? Please translate, I don't speak that language." Alejandro scratched the back of his head.

"It means it reduces infection and numbs the pain." Stella smiled broadly.

"What does it look like? I can go look around." He got up.

"It looks like a rosette of oval green leaves, attached to the root near the ground. The leaves have five parallel veins running from the base of each leaf. The edges and the leaves are smooth. Flowering brownish stalks grow from the center of the rosette." She drew the shapes in the dust with her finger.

"I know exactly which one it is! If you snap the leaf, the veins are very stringy and white inside. I'm on it. Just rest here and we'll fix up this wounded pilgrim in no time." Alejandro took off on his search and returned in just a few minutes skipping and jumping. "I grabbed a few, we can crush some leaves and leave them on the wound. The bigger leaves will be like a bandage holding everything in place. When Philip returns from the creek, he will be so proud you handled your injury!"

He patted her on the back and held the green leaf in place at the bottom of Stella's injured foot.

"What a happy change of mood in the camp! How did you do it, guys?" Philip climbed up the bank of the creek and wrung out the linen cloth dripping with water.

"We used the herbs I read about in *Herbolario*!" Stella sat up straighter. "We just need the kerchief to dry and hold the herbs in place. I should be able to walk on this foot soon."

"Great news! I will spread the cloth out here in the sun." He smoothed out the rough cut of fabric and sat down. "Speaking about books in *templum libri*, I can tell you what I learned about *time* from that astronomy book." Alejandro got comfortable on the ground and Philip continued. "Because the rotational axis of the earth is tilted, over time, a very long time, gravitational influences of the moon and the sun cause a shift in the earth's tilt. Different stars will eventually appear to us in the area of the celestial pole, where Polaris star is now." He pointed his finger up and drew an imaginary circle with his whole hand. "It takes about 26,000 years for the earth's poles to make an imaginary circle in the sky and point to the same area again. Then one travel cycle for the earth is completed."

"Hmmm, a little hard to picture that, but ok." Alejandro furrowed his brow.

"This reminded me that, just like the Romans in the mine, we've been here before in this time of exploiting the environment and not respecting our home planet. Just mining for resources, gold or whatever precious materials everyone needs." Philip crossed his arms on his chest and paced. "Hopefully, when we are back in our time, we can be more mindful of the resources we use and appreciate them."

"Maybe it just takes that long, like 13,000 years, for the people to see the effects of their actions before they can recognize the situation. Before they realize that, collectively, we've been here before – in this space of not caring and plundering the earth, while hurting ourselves in the meantime." Alejandro clenched his jaw.

"What if that's the reason we had these time jump experiences?" Stella rubbed her foot. "To have the opportunity to think differently as the earth is making its cosmic journey and we are along for the ride. We can make a change in the next 13,000 years…"

"Perhaps… As we are walking on this precious ground to our destination, we can remember to be grateful and thankful for everything we receive in our lives so conveniently and easily from the earth."

"Like the herbs we just found for healing my foot! With every step we can count our blessings. Each step can be made in gratitude for the miracle of us being here." She kissed her fingers and pressed them to the ground. "Each breath can be taken in recognition of the magic we see here all through time."

Philip nodded and pressed a hand to his heart. "We can walk and feel supported by the earth, floating in deep space. Let's give thanks for having the comfort of everything we need to call it home."

"Worth a try! The cloth looks dry now, can you help me wrap it tightly so the shoe can fit?" Stella pulled out her sneakers and carefully slid her foot in. She tentatively put her weight on the bandaged foot. "This will work!"

"With this mindset, we will get over those mountains in no time!" Philip patted his sister on the back. "You can ride Tiago for a while, let me lift you up. You are featherlight compared to Artur!"

"This is comfy! I could get used to riding and being in the lead. Do we have any apples?" She rummaged in the saddlebag. "There is some parchment paper here. Did you guys put it here?" Stella pulled out a folded flimsy paper with brownish edges. "The handwriting is very ornate, with ink…"

"What does it say?" Philip perked up.

"*There was a time when all beings were free. Before the false conceptions overloaded the humans who now drag themselves and their possessions on the road of their reality.*" Stella licked her lips. "*The magic is always there, available to change that mindset and create the reality of peace and beauty, unburdened by possessions and heavy thoughts. Leave the non-essential behind – it's too heavy and painful to drag along.*"

"Interesting… anything else?" Alejandro petted Tiago's face.

"*As one foot falls in front of the other on the path to seeking the truth, the burdens become lighter and lighter. The mystery of the ancient path will call strongly to walk immense distances with just a few necessities on the back.*"

"Where did this come from?" Philip scrutinized the delicate paper.

"Another puzzle to ponder and solve in time!" Stella pursed her lips and patted Tiago's neck. "Come on, boy! Santiago is waiting."

Loving the Enemy   15

Fog drifted over the hills and the sun hid somewhere behind the clouds. In this rural part of Galicia, it was hard to tell in what time period the pilgrims walked. Freshly tilled earth, cow pastures and fields could have been there for centuries, if not thousands of years. Not much seemed to change as the farmers tended to their plots of land in such a natural way, not overpowering the surrounding landscape. They worked hand in hand to grow whatever crops they needed and to support the cattle.

The same stone houses stood along the Way in hamlets as constructed in the times of Knights Templar. The young travelers now appreciated the Knights' role in protecting the pilgrims from various perils. They didn't see the horse-mounted patrol that day and all the sleepy villages they passed didn't give away the time either. Gloom descended as the pilgrim crew emerged from the forest of eucalyptus and pine. They came to a fork in the path but didn't see any guiding yellow arrows.

"Luckily, we've seen the arrows until recently and we're heading in the right direction, towards Santiago, no matter what century it is." Stella adjusted the wrap on her injured foot.

"I hear some voices, somewhere behind us. Look, three people are over there." Artur motioned in the direction of the forest. "They have light hiking pants, T-shirts, hiking boots and backpacks – definitely modern clothing, no leather sandals, tunics or swords. They must also be pilgrims on their Way to Santiago."

"Buen Camino," a man said as the newcomers caught up to them.

"Buen Camino!" Philip waved his hand. "This greeting has been with the pilgrims ever since the Middle Ages."

"Well, now we know *when* we are, not so much *where* we are." Even though the newcomers seemed friendly, Stella had an uneasy feeling. There was no one else in sight in these mysterious lonely woods. Are they a possible threat? But why? She couldn't ignore her intuition even when she tried to smile to them.

"Hola peregrinos! Have you seen any arrows? Let's take a photo!" The man pulled out a camera from his pocket.

"How is your walking today?" Philip huddled with the group for the selfie shot and smiled. "Stella, want to be in the picture?"

"No thanks. I can take another one for you." She glanced at the screen and pressed the button without counting out loud, handed the camera back and led Tiago with her eyes fixed on the ground.

"What's up? Is something wrong?" Alejandro caught up to her.

"Something about them… Can't put my finger on it, but something doesn't feel right. It's like they were robbers or bandits in another time. One is bold and missing some teeth. The one with wavy dark hair is so loud. The eyes of the guy with a short hair keep darting in every direction." She quickened her steps.

"I haven't noticed anything strange in their appearance. They are just pilgrims." Alejandro shrugged.

"Still, why are they following us? They said they were unsure which way to go, but maybe it's a plot." She shuddered as the rowdy obnoxious laughter pierced the softness of the fog and disturbed the gentle smell of eucalyptus still lingering in the air.

"Doesn't bother me if they walk behind us, they seem friendly." He peeked over his shoulder. "They fell farther behind, if that worries you less." Alejandro walked on as the path curved and narrowed around a bend. Short stone walls delineated someone's land and a house appeared just around the corner. Bouts of strange metallic grinding noise came from somewhere behind the house, as they approached. A very tall man stepped around the stone wall with a big knife in a hand raised high. Philip halted and pushed Stella back.

"Oh boy! – we're trapped! The guy with a knife in front, stone walls on each side and three robbers behind." Stella's heart pounded. A plausible escape scenario rushed to her head. "Let's push Tiago forward to break the way upfront and incite Tiger to attack. He can scratch at least one of the bandits..." Her eyes darted in all directions. Suddenly, a ray of sunshine broke through the clouds. Stella squinted and somehow noticed the farmer's lips. He was smiling. Maybe he is not so bad after all...

"Good day," Stella said. Worth a try even if he is trying to lure us in.

"*Buenas dias!*" The butcher turned his head slightly and lowered his hand.

"He wasn't going to stab anyone with his humongous butcher knife." Philip relaxed his grip on Stella's arm. "He just sharpened it on the stones and raised his hand to shield his eyes from the sun, to look at us."

"In another time and space, this could have been a very dangerous situation. No wonder the Templars protected the pilgrims in situations where they risked life and limb on their way to Santiago." Stella's heart beat so fast, she had to catch her breath. She watched the "bandits" approach from the corner of her eye.

"Señor, we haven't seen the yellow arrows for a while and wonder if this is the right direction." The "bandit" shook the butcher's hand.

"Yes, just follow this path until a split. The arrows reappear there. A recent storm toppled some trees and knocked over a few stone markers in the area. There is a nice café soon after where you can get some refreshments." With his fearsome knife, the butcher pointed in the direction of the next village with a few stone houses in a distance and patted Tiago on the nose. "Buen Camino, peregrinos!"

Stella felt a little more at ease. Besides, what choice did they have except to keep walking with that gang near them. But she'd keep her guard up.

More sun's rays broke through the clouds as they marched past the neatly kept land plots of potatoes and collard greens.

The first crudely drawn yellow arrow soon appeared on the corner of a stone wall. In a few minutes, they saw a café with a nice patio and a grapevine above the tables. Rose bushes in the garden smelled so good.

"I miss our home… Looks cozy!" Stella opened a little gate.

"It's nice, just as the not-so-butchery farmer told us." Alejandro winked at her.

"Welcome!" The owner showed them a good place to tie Tiago and brought him a bucket of water. "Here is a nice green patch of grass your horse can munch on." He looked at Tiger, but he didn't say anything. The cat settled on Philip's lap as everyone enjoyed tasty warm vegetable soup and fresh bread. The "bandits" pulled up a table to join theirs with happy smiles. Somewhere over the course of the meal, Stella's back and shoulders relaxed. She even enjoyed the laughter from the three funny guys. They didn't annoy her anymore. Their Camino walking mishaps were funny! She even triumphantly shared her herbal medicine foot healing story, from the present time Camino.

"How did you know what herbs to look for?" A man with curly hair sipped on his water, without ice. Ice wasn't common in local drinks.

"I read it in a book once." She became pensive again with a bite of bread in her mouth. Something changed in time, forward and back. Maybe they were robbers back then. Maybe things changed because we weren't afraid to keep walking this time, even though they came out from that mystic forest. Maybe in another time they could mean big trouble. This time we gave them a chance to be their best selves. Maybe she wasn't so friendly at first, but she did give them a chance. They did help us all by asking for directions. The supposed enemy turned out to be quite good company at lunch. Who could have imagined…?

After the meal, laughs and hugs and *buen Camino* wishes, the guys went ahead. Stella checked her foot as the bold man came back. "Here, this must have fallen out from the saddlebag." He handed her a folded brownish sheet of parchment paper and spun around towards the exit. "*Buen Camino!*"

"But…" She stared at the familiar handwriting. When she lifted her head, he was gone. "Guys, come here." She handed the letter to Philip.

"*Santiago and its basilica welcomed many pilgrims. Some walk farther west to Finisterre on the Atlantic coast to watch the sunset over the ocean and to plunge in the unknown world of mysteries and magic.*

"*The sun's setting rays reflecting on the ocean feed the lifeforce of each pilgrim. They bring the sense of purpose beyond the daily tasks. They wake the divine inspiration within and make this world a reality of peace.*

"*The comfort of having a quiet time in the mind. - The ability to dream the life we came here to live. - The satisfaction of fulfilling a destiny. - The joy of looking at the destination of a journey.*

"*If this task along ancient cobblestones can be achieved, absolutely anything can be achieved.*" Philip put the letter down and gazed around.

"What do you make of this?" Alejandro leaned over his shoulder. "The handwriting is so unusual. Nobody writes longhand anymore, much less with these kinds of squiggles and curlicues."

"The paper is very frail, but the edges are surprisingly unworn." Philip lifted the paper up. "Nothing else shows through in the light... Let's keep it safe with the other one. We can figure it out later."

Precious Message 16

The climb to O Cebreiro didn't come easily. George told them that a little village of just a few houses was situated at this high point on the Camino. The uphill wasn't very steep, but the path wound up and up. Rainwater and people's feet had worn out and smoothed the stones to a shine in some places. In others, the rivets of water trickled down along the path. Tiago lost his footing a few times and Tiger nearly slipped out of Stella's hands. "It will be safer for you in a shoulder bag, my fur ball."

"George said that the mountains separated two provinces. We are leaving Leon and entering Galicia. All the plants are so lushly green! And look at all these colorful wildflowers sprinkled on the hillsides." Stella squeezed Tiger a little tighter.

"That means we're getting closer and closer to Santiago!" Alejandro jumped over a puddle and high fived Artur.

"The mountains create their own weather systems and attract rain in the summer and lots of snow in the winter. Not a good place to be caught in bad weather! Imagine, some pilgrims still take this path in the winter." Philip exaggerated lifting his feet high, trudging through imaginary snow. "Now the only inconvenience is having to put on and take off their jackets every half hour."

"The clouds are so temperamental." Alejandro pulled his jacket off and tied it around his waist. "The temperatures definitely drop in the shade. I sure hope we can find some shelter at the village for the night." The rain clouds and blue skies traded places consistently as the wind blew in from the west. The farther they ascended, the more beautiful the views impressed them. The valley unfolded below the hills splattered in patches of yellow flowering bushes, like the leftover splatter from sunny lemon-yellow paint container.

"The scent of green grass and flowers is so much fresher here. Aaahhh…" Stella drew in a breath full of the mountain aromas. "Gonna save some of this lavender for tea."

"Because it rains on and off, the air is saturated with moisture, making all the colors and fragrances more intense." Philip caught Artur just in time as he slipped on a rock. "Are you getting tired? Maybe you can trade places with Stella for a while. Hang on tight in the saddle and hold Tiger. I will lead him slowly." He lowered Stella and gave Artur a lift.

Stella got down and stretched her legs. "Tiger keeps a watchful eye on everyone! Good kitty." She blew him a kiss as the fur ball got comfortable in a bag in Artur's lap.

"The incline isn't so bad as I expected, maybe because we started early from the foothills. That last village, Las Herrerías, probably got its name from a metalsmith who worked there in the past." Alejandro kept up a good speed behind Tiago.

"Now it's such a quiet place. Love all the roses in their gardens." Stella pulled out a pink rose bud she picked from the ground earlier. "It's so gentle and smells so good." She closed her eyes for a moment.

The rain rolled in as they neared the top of the hill. Stella hoped shelter was nearby. They increased the pace and soon saw three horses tied to trees along the path and a stone house nearby.

"Looks like a storage place with hay and other things but no one is nearby. Are those bagpipes?" Stella stood still and listened. "Where are they coming from?"

"Definitely sounds like bagpipes. I wonder what time frame we're in now…" Philip said.

"The Celtic presence in Galicia was very strong in the old days. Maybe the village at O Cebreiro was a former Celtic settlement. Though I heard they play bagpipes even in modern times," Alejandro said as they entered a small village of about ten houses along both sides of cobblestone road. Some houses were square with slate roofs covered by soft moss. A few were round *pallozas*, circular stone houses with roofs of tightly layered straw and tied on top like a braid running across the peak, dividing the circle in two uneven halves.

A man, dressed in a loose tunic, played the bagpipes in the doorway of the palloza, just out of the rain. He didn't look surprised to have strangers approach him. Many pilgrims must have passed his village. Their clothes probably appeared like something from some faraway country. "Come in, come in." The man motioned to them to enter. "My name is Paco, what are your names?"

"My name is Philip. This is my sister, Stella and my brother, Artur." He shook Paco's hand. "Alejandro is our friend. Tiago and Tiger accompany us on the way to Santiago." Philip lowered his head as he stepped through the doorway.

The house seemed much roomier inside than it appeared from the outside. It opened up and gained extra height as large beams rose to the center of the structure. Only a few small windows with wooden shutters let the light in through a round opening cut into each shutter. Once their eyes adjusted to the dim lighting, they could see the same dark gray construction stone as the wall didn't have plaster. Large slick slate slabs created a sturdy floor.

A heavy-set stone oven was built into the wall but didn't appear to be in use when they entered. The fire burned just in front of it, on the floor in the central room. Something smelled delicious in a pot hanging over the fire. "You are welcome to eat and sleep here. Tiago can join the other horses in the barn. Please feel comfortable. Another room with sleeping quarters is on a side." Paco left them to tend to the fire.

"He sounds kinda different." Alejandro sat down on a wooden bench near the fire.

"He speaks Gallego, a local language that developed from Latin, along with Spanish and Portuguese." Philip stretched out his legs. "We can understand him mostly because we speak Spanish; these languages are closely related. Though, Gallego is unique and distinct."

"Look on that platform above, there is more room for storage. Interesting design." Alejandro examined a platform on a side made from heavy wooden beams.

"Here is some warm soup for you, *caldo gallego*. It has potatoes, white beans and local leafy greens. Enjoy!" Paco handed them bowls of steaming soup and slices of fresh bread.

"So yummy!" Artur dug in first.

"I've seen these tall leafy plants in people's gardens in the foothills of the mountains. I wondered what they use them for. Now we have a chance to taste them." Stella blew on the steaming spoon. "This bread is amazing!"

"Glad you like it!" Paco smiled. "The soup is very warming when it gets chilly. The weather changes frequently here. It will be sunny very soon."

"Can I take care of your horses today? We are grateful for the excellent hospitality you offered us." Philip finished the last of his soup and wiped the bowl with a piece of bread.

"I appreciate your offer to help. I'll show you the barn. The rain just let up." Paco and Philip walked out into a gentle mist blown in by the wind. While Philip brushed the horses, filled up their food and water, tidied up the stables, Stella and the boys explored the village.

"Some houses have intricate symbols. This one looks like a spiral or circular labyrinth. That one, like a triangle with a wavy spiral extending from each of the three corners of a triangle. Curious what they are for." Alejandro ran his finger over the woodcarving. "Let's walk up to the little hills around the village for better views of the valley."

"So calm, quiet and peaceful..." Stella took in the view. "These meadows are perfect for a game of tag. You're it!" Stella touched Artur's shoulder and ran off. When it started drizzling again, everyone gathered back in the palloza around the fire.

"Paco, can you tell us about the symbols people use on their houses?" Alejandro sat down next to the host.

"The spiral symbol relates to the search for truth or a inner learning journey." Paco spread the coals with a metal stick and gazed at the lively flickering flames. "The triangle symbol reminds people about the balance of body, mind and spirit. All those components need to be joined for a happy and healthy life."

"How do you do that? Practically, I mean." Alejandro shifted on the tough wooden bench.

"Different people have different ways to achieve that balance. Some take a long journey on the Way, to the top of the hill to this village and even farther after that." Paco smiled gently at Alejandro. "It helps them to stay active, focused and to have a connection of their spirit with nature and the beauty around them." He got up to pick up another log from the pile of wood stacked against the wall.

"We noticed today that your village is so calm and peaceful." Stella looked up from the flames.

"Whatever peace you found here, you brought with you." Paco put another log in the fire, and it hissed as the flames enveloped it. "Through the process of being mindful and setting time aside to reflect on things, you can feel at peace." He put some water from a bucket in a kettle and hung it over the fire. "When your mind, body and spirit are happy, peace and beauty become more apparent."

"Sounds so simple…" Philip petted Tiger on the bench next to him.

"That's the secret of the spiral and the search for truth." Paco winked. "You had it in you all along. You just had to allow the magic to happen, to see it as you walk and pay attention to things."

"Wow!" Alejandro folded his hands on his lap. "We had this calm and magical feeling all along? We walked so far to find something that is always present?!"

"Now you know." Paco beamed. "Who would like some tea? I picked the herbs from the meadows here. Good to add the lavender you gathered for a calm sleep."

"The clouds cleared up. Want to sit outside and look at the stars?" Alejandro touched Stella's shoulder. Her eyes were firmly fixed on the flames. She took her teacup and followed him outside to a little stone ledge outside the front door.

"This is amazing, the stars are so bright and countless." Stella warmed her hands on the cup.

"I wondered in what ways magic would appear to us." Her friend gazed at the stars, so numerous on the dark cozy blanket of the sky above them.

"Look, that star is flickering." Stella swished the aromatic tea around her cup and took a sip.

"I will make a wish then to see more magic on the Way. To find more mysteries in this beautiful land that speaks more and more clearly to me each day." Alejandro touched his heart and raised an open palm to the sky.

"To more wonder-full ways to appear as we approach Santiago!" Stella raised her cup and finished her tea.

"Let's head back. Philip and Artur are already curled up." Alejandro ran his hand along the wall and carefully made his way in the dark.

"These straw mattresses smell so sweet of summer, flowers and new adventures. Good night," Stella whispered as she drifted off to a dreamland in her cot near her brothers.

Santiago on the Horizon 17

Leaving O Cebreiro in the early morning fog was one of Stella's favorite Camino moments so far. They picked up Tiago from the barn on the way out. In this fog, they resembled those mysterious animals from the books in the Templar library. The outline of the horse with Artur and the cat in his hands was hardly recognizable in the obscure morning light.

"What would they call us – *peregrino tigersaurus*? Would sure be scary for anyone to bump into us this time of day." Stella laughed and zipped her jacket.

"A functional arrangement that got us this far." Philip surveyed his crew and adjusted his backpack.

"You said the word *time* again…" Alejandro frowned and glanced over his shoulder.

"Well, let's hope that gets us back on track." Stella slipped her hands into her pockets and gazed ahead. Curiously, on the Camino they really couldn't tell *time*.

The gravel path meandered through the forest. Patches of fog stuck on the big paw-like branches of the pine trees. The rest of the fog floated down in small valleys between the hills. Some scraps stuck closer to the hilltops. Some eventually descended to the ground and turned into morning dew, nourishing the poppies and the lavender plants along the trail. This side of the mountains in Galicia appeared wetter and greener, in the special Galician hue. A special charm burst out from every plant nourished with all the moisture.

"Then out came the sun and dried up all the rain!" Stella jumped into a small puddle sending shiny droplets all around.

"Itsy bitsy spider climbed up the spout again." Alejandro pretended to climb up a pine tree but didn't make it very far up the thick branchless trunk.

"Or not…" Artur laughed from his observation point atop Tiago. "Hey, what's that bright flash down there?" He pointed downhill.

"Seems like the sunlight is reflecting off some glassy surface from what I can tell." Philip shielded his eyes.

"A tractor! That's pretty cool! The design seems to be close to our modern times." Alejandro jumped and clapped his hands.

"Artur, want to take a break and "drive" a tractor?" Philip extended a hand, and everyone ran over to the green machine.

Artur climbed into the cabin and turned the steering wheel. "Vroom, vroom, beep, beep! Out of the way, pilgrim load coming through!"

"Driving would be easier for sure, but then we wouldn't see all the things we see by slow walking." Philip examined the huge tires of the tractor and their thick tread.

"We sure are slow!" Stella laughed, skipped and danced.

"Funny but true!" Alejandro spun her around.

"Hey dancing people, from what I recall hearing about this area, the monastery in Samos is probably a good place to spend the night." Philip gazed over the hills where the path meandered. "We are technically heading down from the mountains, but there will be some up and down over these hills."

"Let's hope we arrive in some century after it was built." Alejandro wiggled his eyebrows.

"You funny!" Stella burst out laughing.

"Watching all the tricks you and Artur pull at home, you are pretty funny yourself!" Alejandro snorted.

"Come on, goofballs. Not sure how far we have to walk to the monastery." Philip lifted his pack back on and boosted Artur into the saddle.

The view of the monastery sprawled unexpectedly through a clearing in vegetation after a turn. The elegant structure fit right in on the green cushions of surrounding lush greens. It glowed like a sparkling jewel with two cloisters of different sizes, three stories tall, encompassing graceful inner courtyards and gardens. The luminous church laid out in a shape of a cross featured a tall bell tower. A stately slate roof covered all areas along the perimeter of the monastery.

"Wow, it looks pretty big! I heard that it's one of the largest monasteries in Europe. It's very old too. It was first occupied in the 6th century," Philip said.

They descended through the village of Samos along a shaded path with ferns, bushes and chestnut trees on one side and a high stone wall on another. The stone houses must have been built centuries ago, but the signs of the modern times were abundant. Everyone laughed and traded high-fives, passing cars and motorcycles parked in the asphalt driveways under the windows with painted acrylic frames and potted geranium flowers on the windowsills. They crossed a small bridge over a calm river Sarria, flowing right under the abbey windows, and circled around the monastery.

"Look, that large door is open!" Artur touched a heavy ornate wooden door.

"Good day!" A monk in loose robes tied around his waist stood up from a chair to greet them.

"Hello, we are pilgrims. Could we stay here for the night?" Philip stepped in but gestured to everyone to stay outside with Tiago.

"Certainly!" The monk got the ink pad and a stamp from a small desk. He placed a large blue stamp in everyone's credential. Monasterio de Samos appeared inscribed above the circle with four images in it. Philip leaned over as the monk wrote the date under each stamp and wiped his forehead.

"Can we get inside the monastery for a look?" Stella peaked in through the open door.

"Yes, you can. Please ask around the village first about lodging for your horse and cat. We can't accept them, unfortunately." He smiled apologetically. "The library is off limits though. Various large fires over the centuries damaged different areas of the monastery. The work of rebuilding and repairing the affected areas was immense, took a long time and spanned many eras. You are welcome to stay for the service at the church later this evening."

They situated Tiago and Tiger for the evening with a lovely family and went to visit the monastery, but not before buying some tasty chocolate at the gift shop.

"Whew! Seems correct!" Philip examined the receipt with a printed date and time of the purchase. "Though we've been walking for quite some time now, we still don't know how the time jumps happen."

"Or how we got those letters…" Stella broke off a piece of milk chocolate.

"The answer seems to be just to keep walking and everything gets lined up as it should." Alejandro stuffed a large chocolate chunk in his mouth.

Inside, they walked in the cloister galleries with stunning vaults and archways open to the inviting courtyard they saw from the top of the hill. "It says here Romanesque, Gothic, Renaissance and Baroque architectural elements are present in different parts of the complex," Stella read.

"That's so unique because most structures are built with one style of the time of its founding." Philip watched the high ceiling and noticed a shell, symbol of the Camino, in one of the vaults.

"It's so impressive that this is a functioning monastery, home to monks of various ages, spending their lives in contemplation and prayer." Alejandro stepped out into the courtyard and gravel crunched under his feet as he walked between the manicured rows of boxwood, palm trees and fruit trees towards a two-tiered fountain. He spooked a tiny bird from a hydrangea bush. It settled on the edge of the top tier and took a sip of water. Its chirps echoed somewhere deep in the galleries. "I can see how this place would inspire philosophers and theologians."

"They said we can see the replica of the great pharmacy that was once located here." Stella started walking down the gallery. "Check this out!" Stella spun around. "Imagine all the herbs and potions and remedies that were available back then. So cool! Look at all those special jars and containers!" Stella wanted to stay in the intriguing room with all the artifacts so much longer, but everyone pressed on to visit the church.

The interior of the church was very open and luminous. Stone pillars reached to the high dazzling ceiling. White stucco walls brightened the spaces even more. The light from the cupola above shined on the statues of marble angels floating above the altar.

"Such a masterpiece! Everything here looks so divinely inspired!" Alejandro turned slowly with his mouth open. He looked at the dome where the four naves joined and counted eight stone supporting curves coming together at the center. "That must be where the bell tower is…"

"How much is five plus seven?" Artur asked.

"Twelve. Why?" Alejandro turned around.

"I am adding these numbers right here but don't have enough fingers." Artur stretched out his hands and spread his fingers.

"You are gonna need so many more fingers because look at all these numbers carved in the stones on the floor, guys!" Alejandro barely stifled his voice.

"Cool!" Philip walked over. "They seem to be placed in certain sections on each side of the pews along the church walls, but closer to the middle, lengthwise." He paced from one side to another. "It looks like a sequence on each side, but not all stones have a number. Then they stop for some reason."

"Is this a secret message?" Alejandro's eyes lit up.

"It could be a numerical message or just a coincidence." Philip sat down in a pew. "Hmmm, in all the timeframes we visited, the languages seemed to be different. Yet the language of math is used very consistently. Wouldn't surprise me if the kind of message meant to be understood by everyone is written in a numerical language."

"Even then, we can only understand some truths and messages when we reach a certain level of growth." Alejandro sat in front of Philip and turned to him. "For example, a very young child doesn't even know yet what the numbers are used for and what they represent."

"We could have the greatest mystery spelled out right in front of us on the floor of this beautiful church." Philip got up and walked over to the stone with number 42. "If we are not ready to process and comprehend it, it will just look like random numbers the workers forgot to chisel out when the construction had been completed." He turned to the sound of a slight rustle on a side.

"Hi, I am Ann." A lady they hadn't noticed before stepped around one of the columns. I'm also a pilgrim, from Denver."

"Nice to meet you." Philip shook her hand. "Our family is originally from Colorado. What a small world."

"I couldn't help but overhear your conversation. I thought perhaps this is a reminder to everyone to seek higher knowledge and inspired learning." Ann leaned her trekking poles on the side of the pew. "That all life's greatest mysteries can become available to us with time, like interpreting these numbers carved in stone."

"But we wouldn't even notice these numbers here if we hadn't walked on the Camino into this church after having been through the experiences we had so far." Stella came out from the nave and stood near Ann.

"True. To even ask this question of what these numbers represent, we have to walk the walk." Ann tapped her index finger on her lip.

"Um… How do you know what questions to ask in the first place?" Alejandro paced around the 0 stone.

"That's a really good thought because these things are so personal and different for everyone. Realizing that there is so much we don't know is the first step." Ann placed her hand on his shoulder. "Staying open to receiving answers to the unknown questions is key." She looked into his eyes. "Add that to walking through life with love and gratitude and watch all kinds of mysteries unfold in their own time and space."

"What I learnt so far is that there is our timing and then there is divine timing when everything unfolds just as it should," Alejandro said softly.

"Maybe the answers are in Santiago or even beyond." Ann picked up her poles and tugged on her backpack strap.

"We set a goal to reach Santiago and it is on the horizon, getting closer every day with all our efforts." Philip pumped Alejandro's fist. "We will rest well tonight!"

"Maybe we meet again in Santiago! I will continue walking to the next town now. Buen Camino!" Ann pulled down her visor and waved on her way out.

"Guys!" Alejandro picked something from the ground near the bench leg. "Looks familiar…" He unfolded the brownish paper. "*When you have a goal, go forward and have faith that everything is exactly as it should be. Your intention puts you exactly at the right place at the right time for magical adventurous experiences.*"

"We are making quite a collection of these inspirational thoughts." Stella placed it carefully in a stack with the other papers and slid it in her backpack. "Gotta find out where they are coming from…" She looked around but the church was empty and silent.

Ending the Quest   18

After few more days of walking, their goal was in sight. They topped the Monte de Gozo – the Mountain of Joy – and reached the city limits. They could see spires of the cathedral from many different streets as they headed to Santiago's medieval center. The bustling city jarred them after the quiet of the smaller rural towns and the countryside. It was the modern Santiago where people rushed about either by foot or in cars. Horns honked, people in suits went to work, others engrossed in their cellphones – either in conversations or deeply focused on the screens. The sights, the sounds, the smells of a working city with a flavor of car exhaust invaded the senses.

They saw other pilgrims identifiable by their hiking clothes, backpacks with the scallop shells but mostly by their happy faces. A little bewildered by all the ruckus descending on them after days or weeks of peaceful walking. They all streamed like ants to their home, from different directions of various Camino routes. They all streamed determinately to the Plaza de Obradoiro with Santiago Cathedral – the goal of their lengthy quests. Their drive and speed increased with the proximity to the fulfillment of their dreams to reach the magnificent cathedral of Santiago.

The young pilgrims followed the signs to the Pilgrim's Office first where a line of people formed to receive their Compostela certificates upon completion of their journeys. Stella found a volunteer greeting the pilgrims. "Hello! We are looking for Sister Maria who volunteers here at the office."

"Head upstairs and knock on the second door on the left. If she is not there, come to me and I will try to find her for you." The woman motioned towards the stone steps.

"Thank you so much!" Stella shot upstairs first. She knocked on the open door.

A beautiful simply dressed lady with a touch of gray in her hair came to greet them. "Hello pilgrims! Please come in! I am Sister Maria." She smiled warmly and invited them in. "Welcome! Please tell me your names."

"I am Stella. My brothers are Artur and Philip. This is my friend Alejandro. This is our cat Tiger." She opened up her shoulder bag a little wider. "He is scared of all the city commotion."

"Nice to meet you all!" Tiger licked Sister Maria's hand as she petted him.

"Actually, that's not all. Our horse Tiago is outside. We saw some police officers on horseback, they said they would watch him and they know a place to house him for the night." Artur looked out the window. "I can see him right there. Some pilgrims are talking to him."

"Sister Maria," Philip cleared his throat. "The main reason we walked the Camino is to deliver this letter personally to you." He fished out the special letter from his inner pocket. "From Alejandro's grandfather." The envelope appeared a little tattered, but the seal stayed intact, just like the Grandfather put it. Philip handed it to the nun and plopped down on a chair. "Whew! Feels like all those stones we passed on the way had dropped from my shoulders…"

"We are finally here! Can you believe this?! We delivered this special letter to Sister Maria!" Stella swiped the tear from the corner of her eye.

"He could have a request for you, but we don't know. Nobody peeked at it." Alejandro straightened his shoulders and lifted his chin. "Not once!"

The nun carefully examined the seal and lifted it from the envelope. She put her glasses on, read the letter and left it folded it on her desk. "I see why he didn't want to mail this letter…" She tapped her fingers on the table, placed her glasses on top of the letter and stood up. "Let me think what can be done about this. Thank you for taking this journey to deliver this special note to me."

"It's our pleasure, but it sure wasn't easy!" Artur stepped away from the window.

"I doubt you had a simple journey. But you all are tough! Relax here for a minute, I will be right back." She came back with a tray full of cups with steaming aromatic mint tea and a plate of sugar cookies. "Please enjoy, you earned it!" Sister Maria watched and smiled as they devoured the cookies.

"Mmmm… We haven't had anything sweet since we left the house." Stella savored a crunchy cookie bite.

"So please tell me more about your trip? What interesting things have you discovered in your travels?" Sister Maria folded her hands in her lap and turned to Stella.

"We've been through so much to accomplish this task." Stella focused on her dusty shoes and a scraped knee. "The Knights Templar helped us a lot. We tried to stay away from the Romans, and the Celts at O Cebreiro are very kind."

"The monastery in Samos is a very peaceful place…" Alejandro sighed.

"That's wonderful!" The nun nodded and leaned forward. "Tell me more about your adventures."

"So many magical and special moments to recount." Philip shifted in his chair and sat straighter. "We spent the night alone in the forest one time and weren't scared… mostly not scared."

"We lost our horse and then got lost ourselves. But luckily we found him." Artur smiled broadly.

"Then there was a time Alejandro called in the dragons…" Philip leaned in.

"Not sure how that happened." Alejandro blushed.

"Really? Sounds incredible!" Sister Maria tilted her head.

"You know, we were wondering the whole way… What is so important in the letter?" Stella lowered her voice. "Do we need to bring a message back?"

"Oh Yes! The message was very important," the nun said and put her reading glasses back on. "Here is what the letter says:

Dear Sister Maria,
Please give the kids some cookies.
They walked a long way from home to Santiago.
Thank you and warm regards,
Jose Francisco"

Stella swallowed, Philip stared at the letter, Alejandro swallowed, and Artur sat down. "We walked all this way to get cookies?!" Artur put both hands on his hips and burst out laughing.

"Apparently!" The nun placed her hand on Stella's shoulder and looked directly into her eyes. "You see now, not only the destination matters. The journey and how you get here are very important too. You had a goal and you walked with open hearts. You listened to your intuition and created magic along the Way."

"How we got here is key. We certainly changed a few timeframes and places on this journey!" Stella beamed.

"Amazing adventures rewarded you because you are determined and brave. Know that you are enough. When you are connected to the divine, what you do is enough to create magic in your lives," Sister Maria said softly.

Stella nodded. "All the effort we put into this journey was worth it." She closed her eyes and savored the tea. "The cookies are sweet, but we received the rewards so many times already." She sipped the last of the fragrant mint tea. "Thank you for your kindness to us and your service to all pilgrims."

"My pleasure. What a special treat it is to meet you all. Don't forget about the pilgrims' mass at the cathedral later this evening. Buen Camino, pilgrims!"

"We will visit next time we are in Santiago!" Stella blew a kiss and headed downstairs.

"What do we do now?" Philip ran his hand through his hair and tugged on the ends.

"Our fearless leader looks lost…" Stella touched his elbow and rubbed his shoulder.

"Kinda. I feel dazed. Now that we're here, it's very surreal." He sat down on a stone edge of the fountain in the courtyard. "Guess, we'll pick new goals from here…"

"It's a lot to process for all of us. Come on, let's get something to eat." Alejandro pulled on Philip's arm to get up.

"I noticed a café selling crepes on the way here. It smelled really good." Stella licked her lips. "The strawberry jam would be an awesome treat."

"I saw it too." Alejandro's eyes widened. "They had tables outside, which is good for going with Tiger. Hope they have something for him too."

"Will be a great time to recollect and celebrate! We did it!" Philip opened his arms, and everyone jumped in to hug him.

"Let's have fun now! We earned it!" Artur skipped from cobblestone to cobblestone up the street. They didn't have to walk far. The cathedral spire still loomed above the houses in the historic city center. The stone buildings in the old city stood wall to wall with the ground floor framed by the arches and open to the restaurants and storefronts. They mingled with the locals and checked out the window displays along a pedestrian street full of shops selling cheeses, souvenirs, handmade goods, seafood and home décor items. People strolled around or felt the clothing on the display racks outside the stores. Women tried on straw summer hats, wrapped the scarves over their shoulders and touched the purses.

"I want to buy bracelets with the Camino shell for Mama and Papa." Stella saw a jewelry store. "Maybe your Grandpa would like something too." She pulled Alejandro by the sleeve. "Look, Philip, these match the shell you wear on your chain."

"Yes, those are great. I will get us a table. Catch up when you find something you like." He and Artur moved past a few restaurants and waved to a couple enjoying their dinner at a table outside. The man raised his glass to them as they saw Tiger scoping out the situation from Artur's shoulder bag. Philip smiled and headed to the café with a chalkboard outside that spelled out *Crepes* in large letters.

"We should get a table outside too. This one is great." Philip pulled up a chair. "It's still protected by the roof of the gallery just in case it rains. We can still see everyone on the street through these large arches."

"Goof afternoon!" A waitress came over with the menus. "What would you like to drink?"

"We are expecting two more people. We will take two freshly squeezed orange juices for now and a little milk in a bowl for our cat, please. Here they come! Thanks!"

"Hello!" Stella settled into a chair and put the gift bag on the table. "I'd like some lemonade, please. We are celebrating!"

"Of course! What are you celebrating?" The waitress jotted down the order.

"We just completed our Camino! This calls for raspberry iced tea." Alejandro pulled out his pilgrim credential and showed the last stamp received at the Pilgrim's Office. He spelled out the words *Catedral de Santiago*.

"Congratulations! That's exciting! I will be right back with your drinks. Our daily specials are on the back of the menus." She stepped inside and returned in a flash with a tray full of drinks. "Here you go, kitty." She poured some milk in a bowl for Tiger.

"Let's keep him close, away from the sidewalk. Many people are walking with their dogs." Stella moved her chair a little. "I just saw a huge Saint Bernard and a pretty poodle." Tiger lapped up his milk.

"What would you like to order?" The waitress had her pen and notepad ready.

"We will all have crepes. Banana and hazelnut spread for me, strawberries and whipped cream for Stella, apples and cinnamon for Alejandro, and cheese and mushrooms for Artur. If you have a small piece of salmon for Tiger, he will surely appreciate it. Did I get it right?" Philip looked around the table and raised his glass of orange juice.

"Cheers guys! To the best pilgrim companions ever!" Stella's glass clinked with the others.

"We picked a perfect place. Those guys across the walkway are playing the guitar so nicely." Alejandro gave the musical group two thumbs up. "Great tunes!"

"I miss my guitar. Didn't play it much – we left home so quickly." Philip got up and walked over to the other table to greet them. He returned smiling with an acoustic guitar in his hands. "They let me borrow it for a bit." He placed it on his knee and strummed the cords. "Nice sound. What song would you like to hear?"

"Three Little Birds!" Stella perked up.

"Good choice, little sis. I like this one." Philip ran his fingers over the frets. "Drilled this song in my head. Mom made me practice a million times for our aunt Tanya's wedding. It was a fun wedding though!"

"Mom said everyone enjoyed your performance at the reception. And you were only eight years old!" Artur turned to this big brother. "Let's hear it."

Philip started the first chords of Bob Marley's masterpiece "Don't worry… about a thing…" The guitar owner recognized the melody right away across the walkway and came over with his friends. "'Cause every little thing's gonna be alright!" They tapped to the beat on the table and joined in. "Rise up this morning… Smile with the rising sun!" Passerby stopped to listen and watched the joyful performance with big smiles on their faces. "Three little birds pitched by my doorstep." After final "Every little thing's gonna be alright!" the small crowd cheered and clapped. Philip bowed and handed the guitar to its owner. "Thanks for letting me borrow the guitar. It's been fun!"

"Bravo! Nicely done! We will be playing at our table, come over when you all finish your food." The young man bumped Philip's fist.

"Amazing feeling to be here in the old city." Stella noticed the flickering light of the lanterns lit under the archways while they sang and passed the evening in company and comradery. "Seems about time to head to the pilgrims' mass."

Who Are You?   19

A few minutes' walk took them to the Plaza de Obradoiro where the Romanesque façade of the cathedral soared above all, graced by two ornate towers. They admired the central figure of Santiago (Saint James) and his two disciples, all dressed as pilgrims. They noticed the urn in between, representing the found tomb from the legend Grandfather related. Above, a star shone amidst the angels and the clouds, to symbolize the lights that guided the hermit to the tomb. Wow, now I know what the word breathtaking means, Stella caught her breath and walked up the steps constructed of two ramps in a diamond shape leading to the entrance. From there, she could see the stone pattern spreading from the plaza center in eight rays. Like the warm sun that lit our way here, Stella thought.

They entered Pórtico da Gloria with its three arches decorated with over 200 figures of saints, angels and musicians completed with amazing detail and touching facial expressions. The figure of Santiago, the patron of the cathedral, adorned the central column and welcomed all pilgrims inside. They paid respects to Santiago seated on a chair, supported by two lions, holding a scroll and a staff.

Inside the cathedral, they were amazed by the beauty and simplicity of the lines of the immense structure that seemed to reach all the way to the sky. They spotted the locations of twelve crosses with consecration inscriptions for the cathedral in Latin. On each plaque, the equal-sided cross divided the circular engraving in four parts. Top two quarters depicted reliefs of the sun and the moon. Bottom two showed decorative Greek letters alpha and omega. *I am the Alpha and the Omega, the first and the last, the beginning and the end.* The familiar phrase rang out in Stella's mind.

We are finally here! Stella hugged Philip around his waist, as high as she could reach. She still remembered hugging him just above his knee when she was tiny. Now the big brother trusted her to make this big journey with him! Stella dreamed so much about the Camino sitting at the front step of her home. Yet she couldn't possibly imagine then how magical it turned out in real life. Wow, has she really lived through all that? She admired all the pilgrims who came to mass, many with pensive and reverent looks on their faces. Observing everyone's expressions distracted her from the mass quite a bit. The calm melodic voice of the priest drew her back when he named the home countries of the pilgrims arriving that day – Australia, Spain, Germany, France, Korea, Canada, US, Japan, Ukraine, the list went on. She drifted to the dreamland again until his saying caught her attention – *The Camino continues when you go home. Everyone has come a long way to Santiago, but this is only the beginning.* How memorable and deep, she thought.

Everyone would return to their homes, their families, their communities soon. The pilgrims would carry the love and lessons from the Camino, wherever they went from here. They would bring the experiences from the pilgrimage and implement those in daily lives, to bring more understanding and closeness with other people.

The sweet voice of one of the nuns carried a sacred hymn to all corners of the cathedral. The sound flew up to the rafters and landed on the shoulders of inspired pilgrims. Eight clergymen lowered the *Botafumeiro* on its ancient pulley system from the ceiling. Dressed in maroon-colored robes, they set in motion this immense silver incense burner with about 90 pounds of charcoal and incense, only about half of its unfilled weight. The hymn continued its path around the cathedral as the Botafumeiro rose higher and higher. Each man pulled on ropes attached to the pulley system and slowly got the Botafumeiro in motion, swinging way up high above the heads of pilgrims from one nave of the cathedral to the other. Stella, along with mesmerized crowd, watched and listened as if in a trance. The sweet, pungent, calming smell of smoky incense clouds brought her mind inwards and outwards at the same time. She replayed the details of her Camino. Common, simple, centuries-old questions came up as they manifested every day during the walk with her brothers and friend, but in a different context.

What is your name? Where are you coming from? How far are you going?

The Camino presented itself as the metaphor for the voyage of life. Who are you and what are your experiences so far?

Where did you start your life journey and what defines you as an individual? What are your opinions, background and a place of birth? All this related to where Stella and the pilgrims began their journeys. Now that they had traveled so far and endured so much, the Camino had changed them. Some got their questions answered, some got clues to their next steps. Some were not yet aware of any major changes in their thinking. But they could be assured that deep down, on a cellular level, it worked. The earth responded to the imprint their feet left on the ground with a precious gift of recognition of the efforts taken towards seeking clarity and values in their lives. The gift of divine connection with *all that there is*. They would be forever changed and always have this gift with them. It would only be discernible by the bright sparkle in their eyes and barely noticeable glow of their skin. It would be known in their actions within their communities upon return home. She would hug Mama and Papa so tight when she got home, Stella imagined her arms around her parents.

Then there was the question of how far were they going? Now that they received the inspiration, blessings and clarity of the Camino, what were their goals in life? How far would they go to implement them and make their dreams a reality? What was their purpose here and what steps needed to be taken to achieve it in this world? Stella looked up and all around her, taking it all in, processing the feelings and emotions that suddenly enveloped. Tears flowed down her cheeks freely, but she wasn't sad. She was happy, elated in fact. Wiping down the tears, she noticed others doing the same. They seemed so relieved, but very distant, far in their thoughts and emotions.

The Camino has a special magnetism that seems to activate those ever-present divine seeds in everyone. Now that they felt it, how far would they go to find out who they were and what special gifts and talents they had come to share? *The Camino continues when you return home*, but their home was this entire beautiful world. It was open and waiting for them to walk shining that light for all. When they got home, would they recognize that special sparkle in their eyes, the gentle glow and remember the lessons of the Camino? The sweet incense of the ancient Botafumeiro purified everyone's thoughts, in a way that would help them present the best version of themselves each day.

Now go and know exactly who you are. Stella pressed her fingers to her lips and sent a prayer all the way up with the gentle swirl of the incense smoke.

End of the World 20

Next morning, they wandered through the old town of Santiago and out on the way to the train station, barely talking. Everyone had their own thoughts, coming to terms with the fact that they arrived in Santiago and now got ready to leave. What a journey it had been on the physical Camino trail and on the trail of time on which the timeless Camino took us. Philip noticed his dusty sneakers with a little hole developing on the right side. Their feet walked on gravel, cobblestone, rocks, dirt, mud and now on the asphalt streets of the town that also seems to defy time. The ancient stone walls, the plazas and the cathedral called so many pilgrims over so many centuries.

This must be one of the processes helping people feel their connections with the divine. He watched the fluffy clouds move slowly across the sky. The happy laughs of the children on the playground in Alameda Park resonated with the joy in his heart opening to the light on this beautiful journey. Philip drew in a deep breath and smiled. When the fireworks lit up the Santiago cathedral and Plaza Obradoiro on major holidays, those colors and lights gave thanks for the protection and love felt by the pilgrims, city residents and travelers alike.

"Well, here it is, guys! Remember to pay attention to the stops and get off in the right place. You will be home in just a few hours!" Philip stepped down the stairs leading to Santiago's train station.

"That quick?! We walked all these days when we could have taken the train!?" Artur stared at his brother.

"That's right! Exactly my words when mom and dad took me on my first Camino." Philip laughed. "We do have time for a snack at the café before your train leaves. Come on down."

"I'd like to have a tortilla, a Spanish omelet with potatoes." Stella asked the waitress and climbed up on a chair near the high counter.

"A croissant for me, please." Alejandro sat next to her.

"I just want some French fries and an egg for Tiger." Artur's legs dangled from a tall chair.

"Orange juice for me, please." All other seats along the counter were occupied, so Philip stood behind Stella.

"Good day!" Stella quickly made friends with a man next to her. "My name is Stella. Are you a pilgrim?" She spotted the backpack down at his feet.

"Hi, I'm Randy. Nice to meet you. Yes, I am a pilgrim, from Canada." Randy shook Stella's and Philip's hands. "You look like pilgrims too."

"We just finished in Santiago, but Philip will go on to Finisterre." Stella patted her brother on his back.

"It will take me a while longer to get back since Tiago, our horse, can't get on the train. I will miss these munchkins though…" He took a bite of Stella's tortilla.

"You know, in the old days, pilgrims didn't end their journey in Santiago. They still had to walk back home as you will do." Randy sipped on his coffee, café con leche, many pilgrims' favorite. "Some pilgrims went even farther west before they returned, all the way to the Atlantic Ocean to Cape Finisterre. In Latin, that meant "the end of the world", before the Americas were discovered."

"Are you going to Finisterre?" Stella shifted in her chair.

"I am finished walking for now but will surely be back again." Randy took another sip. "I am taking the train to meet my wife in Rome. We will be celebrating our wedding anniversary there."

"Congratulations! How sweet! Bet you missed each other a lot. She will love to hear all your Camino stories." Stella tugged on a glass in Philip's hand and sipped some of his orange juice.

"What did you think of the Camino, Stella?" Randy asked softly and tilted his head.

"We had a great time, with a few mishaps here and there, but we made it. But I realized something last night…" She put her elbow on the counter and rested her chin on her hand. "When I was at home, watching everyone walk, I just wanted to go too, as soon as I could. But it's not just any kind of walking…"

"How so?" Randy pulled up his chair.

"When we walk in haste or walk weighed down by the burdens, the anxious energy vibrates through our bodies and our feet. Every intense step carries that energy all the way down. How we walk is what we imprint on the earth." Stella moved a sugar packet on the counter around her plate. "We need to have lightness in our step to carry happiness on the earth and it will transmit all the way."

"How will you walk differently when you go home?" Randy squinted and leaned forward.

"I will flutter like a butterfly from one rose bush to another." Stella smiled and touched the butterfly on her dress.

"Still wondering about those letters…" Alejandro scooted over and nudged her. "Show them, maybe Randy will have an idea."

"Here… They look very old and each appeared out of nowhere…" She handed the letters to Randy.

"Hmmm… This could be one of those unsolved Camino mysteries. Camino magic…" Randy tapped his fingers on the counter. "Perhaps, your guardian angels are looking out for you."

"Hate to interrupt…" Philip touched his shoulder. "They just announced your train. Luckily, you can talk more on the train." He leaned over the counter." Can we get the bill, please?"

"I will take care of it. It will be my pleasure." Randy walked over to the register.

"That's so kind of you to treat us." Philip gave everyone a hug. "I will see you all at home! Take care, pilgrims! Don't forget to show all your stamps to Grandpa. Everyone at home will be so proud of you completing this journey." Philip waved from the platform to his pilgrim crew and Tiger in Artur's hands, all smiling behind the window glass of the departing air-conditioned coach. He sat on the platform bench for some time and then went to get Tiago from his host.

"Let's follow the sun to the west, all the way to the ocean, my friend. We will have to go slow within city limits." Philip held the bridle and walked alongside his horse. He thanked the strangers for Buen Camino wishes, the pilgrim shell was still attached to the saddle bag. No more confused and amused looks from the locals – it was just him and the horse now, without the company of his siblings, their friend and the cat. He had fun having them along but could really enjoy his quiet time now. Riding alone or walking along side of Tiago was different from having the whole busy bunch nearby. He needed this contemplative time.

One night sitting outside the barn where Tiago was spending the night, Philip couldn't help but notice the Milky Way above his head. All those stars, swirling above in a special dance from east to west, same direction as he went. *As above and so is below*, the saying goes. He pondered how many other larger cycles happen in nature and are mirrored by our journeys in life on the ground. He wondered how many other pilgrims felt relaxed and connected, resting and getting inspired after the day's walk.

Those stars always seemed to have called people to follow, along the Milky Way. If one could imagine his journey with the stars way up high and then consider that perspective on the earthly journey, they could glean so many revelations from that point of view. They wouldn't give so much significance to the daily quarrels or disappointments. They'd appreciate and revel in the beauty and the miracle of the blue sky and the green earth. They'd see the magic of starlight and they'd discover the nurture of their own sun supporting and holding their home planet.

If they could gain that perspective, the ideas of interconnectedness of all would become more apparent. The dreams of peace would become more real and grounded in their place in space. The knowledge that they have been here in this moment in time could help them be wise to bring more love and light to their daily interactions. Looking at the stars had those kinds of influences on Philip.

Next day was even more magical when he and Tiago reached Finisterre's rugged coast. The lighthouse on the cape provided a perfect place to watch the sunset. The sun completed its journey for the day and went to rest out of sight, below the horizon, way far in the waters of the Atlantic. Its farewell rays lit up the sky with pinks, oranges, and reds of amazing brilliance. As it dipped below the waters, the colors persisted for some time, bouncing off the fluffy clouds and calm waters. Philip finally understood why so many made the extra effort to see this spot.

It's a perfect place to give dreams a little extra brilliance from the sun, with the substance sustained by the strength and support of the earth. The fresh air brings the clarity to the mind to envision the next steps to materialize those dreams. The ocean reminds the pilgrims that one may need to take a boat or think differently to allow those steps to make strong impact.

The iconic lighthouse shined its light so the mariners could find their way home. At the same time, good intentions are projected out far and high, so that all can find the way to their ultimate home. This lighthouse will send them support and light over the ocean and high mountains, so they can shine their bright light to the whole world and see themselves as iridescent precious pearls inside the protective Camino shell.

It may take time to begin realizing why they made this journey, to know the treasure and value of their personal gifts, to learn loving themselves as a special integral part of this world. Their inner glow will grow brighter.

"What a journey, what a way to finish our treasure quest. It's been magical, no doubt. Time to head home tomorrow, my trusted stallion." Philip ran his hand over Tiago's muscular side. "Tonight, is one more night under this field of stars, my friend."

Home Sweet Home 21

A stray ray of sunshine snuck into Stella's room though the light curtains and landed on her cheek. She scrunched up her nose and opened her eyes. "I'm home!" She moved her covers and sat up. "My comfy mattress! My soft pillow, how much I enjoyed my snuggly bed!" She walked over to the window. "Hi birdies!" She ran her hand over the images of the birds on the curtains and spread them open. "Good morning sun!" She pushed the window open and leaned out. All the familiar smells flooded in. Ahhhh - the freshly cut grass with a hint of lilac bush. The grass was so much greener, and the pears have ripened. The leaves on the grapevine really filled in and cast a lovely shade over the patio. A young pilgrim couple enjoyed their coffee in the cozy corner of the garden and added heavy juicy grapes to their morning snack. Had they been gone so long?

She pulled her dresser drawer open. So many fresh clean dresses! *Forgot I have such good taste.* She grinned and pulled out a frilly light violet dress. This will do. "Where is that cat? Is he confused too?" She pattered downstairs to the kitchen. "Mama! Papa!" She flung her arms around them. "I missed you so much!" She slid in on the bench at the table near Artur and Tiger. "How did you sleep, Artur?"

"Best sleep ever! My mattress is so much softer than the ground or those straw mattresses." He cut a piece of a waffle.

Mama raised an eyebrow. "You slept on the ground?"

"We did, but it was perfectly safe. Philip always made sure we were. You would be so proud of him, Papa. He took great care of us." Stella put some apricot jam on her waffle. "Is this from this season? Very tasty."

"How was your Camino? Who uses straw mattresses anymore?" Mama poured tea for everyone.

"It was great! And long story… You won't believe it, we slept in a castle, met the Templar Knights and the Celts, escaped the Romans…" Artur pulled another waffle to his plate. "So much fun!"

"Really?!" Mama pinched his cheek. "Sounds like the Camino was great for your imagination!"

"Definitely for imagination, and for inspiration. And for wonderful peaceful dreams too!" Stella gave Mama a kiss. "It was simply amazing!"

"We got so much support along the Way. Sometimes help came from such unexpected places when we really needed it." Artur glanced at Stella as she tried to hide a smirk on her face. "We had such amazing hosts and awesome food! So important to lift the spirits if someone had a tough walking day. I can now appreciate what you do here at the guesthouse for the pilgrims."

Papa put his fork and knife down. "You both have really matured during this journey. Did you see the Botafumeiro during the mass in Santiago?"

"We did! Quite a sight, very magical. My favorite part during the mass was *Camino continues when you return home.*" Stella put her plate in the sink. "Gonna go see if any pilgrims have any questions about the next walking stretch."

"I'll come along." Artur stood up. "Will be nice to sit on the front steps with you for a change."

"Did Philip say how long he would be? I almost finished the shed but saved a few last pieces for him to nail. He may like to put his touch on it." Papa finished his tea.

"Not sure. He went all the way to Finisterre and then will head back. Should be faster since he has Tiago." Stella glanced at Artur. "He should be back in a flash, without any problems, I hope."

"Finisterre is such a special place." Mama sighed. "I was there with my friends Mar, Emilio, and Aran. It was the first time on the Camino for all of us. We all met while walking and continued as a group. We arrived in Finisterre on a stormy windy day, but it was still magical watching the ocean from the rugged cliffs."

"Sounds nice, Mama. Maybe we can go there again together." Stella picked up the backpack she left on the floor the night before. "Could you please add my things to the laundry? Can't wait for Philip to get back with his stories. Thanks for breakfast!" Stella and Artur took off.

"These clothes have seen better days. But seems like the kids really had fun." Mama smiled. "But look at these papers Stella had in the inner pocket of the pack." She handed them to Papa.

"The paper smells smoky and a little moldy. It's stained in a few places. Here the ink is fading a little. These are really old." He studied the page. "The script is so distinct."

"Almost like a diary of some sort or someone's reflections about the Camino." Mama read a few pages out loud. "*The magic is always there*... Will have to ask them later how they came by to have these."

"Do you believe what they said about the Templars?" He slid the handwritten pages in a book and carefully placed it on the shelf.

"Camino has so many unexplained mysteries and miracles. It's hard to tell sometimes what is real and what is magical." She looked out through the open door at Stella and Artur chatting on the front step. "Nice to have them back home."

A young couple came down the hallway. "We are ready to walk on. Thank you for your hospitality." The man put on his baseball cap and the woman adjusted her floppy hat.

"Good morning! How far are you walking today?" Stella scooted over allowing them to pass.

"Probably about 20 km or so. We are not pushing it today." The man clicked his waist backpack buckle.

"You will have an easy day today, just a few small hills but mostly flat." Stella beamed.

"You sound like you familiar with the trail. Have you walked the Camino?" The woman lifted the brim of her hat.

"Yes, we have! We did it! Just got back last night." Stella high fived her smiling brother.

"That's right all the way to Santiago!" Artur lifted his chin.

"Congratulations! You are very young and brave to go on such a journey! How did you like it?" The lady retied her shoe.

"It really changed the way we see the world, added a new colorful filter." Stella noticed lots of new buds on the rose bush next to the front door. "When you get to Ponferrada, make sure to stop at the castle. It's magical!"

"Thanks for the tips! We will! Ready to go, honey?" The young man rolled up his pant legs and turned to his girlfriend.

"Buen Camino! Enjoy the journey!" Artur waved to them.

"Want to walk over to Alejandro's? Can't wait to hear his new tunes." Stella stood up and offered her hand to Artur. "Can you believe it? We have our own Camino stories to tell Grandpa! When Philip is back from Finisterre, we will enjoy some amazing evenings by the fireside."

"You know, there was so much excitement each day on the Camino and so much going on. Now that we are back home, there are many memories to "unpack" and experiences to mull over." Artur took her hand and spun her around. "I wonder what other magic we will notice right here at home…" He listened to the birds while Stella collected a bouquet of wildflowers on a side of the path. They scooted over to let a group of pilgrims walk by.

"Buen Camino to all!"

ABOUT THE AUTHOR

Elena Skvirski lives in Denver, Colorado. She is the founder of Adventure Camino, a company specializing in supporting pilgrims on the Camino de Santiago in Spain and Portugal. She has walked the Camino on her own as well as with her family and children. Elena is an engaging speaker and enjoys sharing her passion for this ancient journey by presenting, teaching and organizing her local Camino community group. Elena contributes her insights and practical travel knowledge in the videos and on the blog on her website AdventureCamino.com to further assist anyone interested in undertaking the spiritual journey along the Camino.

Adventure Camino Tours
Denver, CO
303.900.4884
info@adventurecamino.com
www.adventurecamino.com

Visit Adventure Camino to discover resources, Camino insights, travel and packing tips, Camino trip planning with help on securing the best accommodations, luggage transport, Camino with children, yoga retreats and much more.

www.ingramcontent.com/pod-product-compliance
Lightning Source LLC
Chambersburg PA
CBHW021107080526
44587CB00010B/421